GUI  ES

GW00691808

/ PART 2

ust 2015

Commissioned by **David Spriggs;** *Edited by*

Guidelines © BRF 2015

The Bible Reading Fellowship
15 The Chambers, Vineyard, Abingdon OX14 3FE
Tel: 01865 319700; Fax: 01865 319701
E-mail: enquiries@brf.org.uk; Websites: www.brf.org.uk; www.biblereadingnotes.org.uk

ISBN 978 0 85746 129 2

Distributed in Australia by Mediacom Education Inc., PO Box 610, Unley, SA 5061.
Tel: 1800 811 311; Fax: 08 8297 8719;
E-mail: admin@mediacom.org.au
Available also from all good Christian bookshops in Australia.
For individual and group subscriptions in Australia:
Mrs Rosemary Morrall, PO Box W35, Wanniassa, ACT 2903.

Distributed in New Zealand by Scripture Union Wholesale, PO Box 760, Wellington
Tel: 04 385 0421; Fax: 04 384 3990; E-mail: suwholesale@clear.net.nz

Publications distributed to more than 60 countries

Acknowledgments

The New Revised Standard Version of the Bible, Anglicised Edition, copyright © 1989, 1995 by the Division of Christian Education of the National Council of the Churches of Christ in the USA. Used by permission. All rights reserved.

The Holy Bible, New International Version (Anglicised Edition), copyright © 1979, 1984, 2011 by Biblica. Used by permission of Hodder & Stoughton Publishers, an Hachette UK company. All rights reserved. 'NIV' is a registered trademark of Biblica. UK trademark number 1448790.

The Holy Bible, English Standard Version, published by HarperCollins Publishers, © 2001 Crossway Bibles, a division of Good News Publishers. Used by permission. All rights reserved.

Scripture quotations marked HCSB are taken from the Holman Christian Standard Bible®, Copyright © 1999, 2000, 2002, 2003, 2009 by Holman Bible Publishers. Used by permission. Holman Christian Standard Bible®, Holman CSB®, and HCSB® are federally registered trademarks of Holman Bible Publishers.

Printed by Gutenberg Press, Tarxien, Malta.

Suggestions for using *Guidelines*

Set aside a regular time and place, if possible, when you can read and pray undisturbed. Before you begin, take time to be still and, if you find it helpful, use the BRF prayer.

In *Guidelines*, the introductory section provides context for the passages or themes to be studied, while the units of comment can be used daily, weekly, or whatever best fits your timetable. You will need a Bible (more than one if you want to compare different translations) as Bible passages are not included. At the end of each week is a 'Guidelines' section, offering further thoughts about, or practical application of what you have been studying.

Occasionally, you may read something in *Guidelines* that you find particularly challenging, even uncomfortable. This is inevitable in a series of notes which draws on a wide spectrum of contributors, and doesn't believe in ducking difficult issues. Indeed, we believe that *Guidelines* readers much prefer thought-provoking material to a bland diet that only confirms what they already think.

If you do disagree with a contributor, you may find it helpful to go through these three steps. First, think about why you feel uncomfortable. Perhaps this is an idea that is new to you, or you are not happy at the way something has been expressed. Or there may be something more substantial—you may feel that the writer is guilty of sweeping generalisation, factual error, theological or ethical misjudgment. Second, pray that God would use this disagreement to teach you more about his word and about yourself. Third, think about what you will do as a result of the disagreement. You might resolve to find out more about the issue, or write to the contributor or the editors of *Guidelines*.

To send feedback, you may email or write to BRF at the addresses shown opposite. If you would like your comment to be included on our website, please email connect@brf.org.uk. You can also Tweet to @brfonline, using the hashtag #brfconnect.

Writers in this issue

Paul Moore is Archdeacon for Mission Development in the Diocese of Winchester. Previously Vicar of St Wilfrid's Church, Cowplain, in Portsmouth Diocese, he was part of a team that created and launched the first Messy Church there in 2004.

Richard Littledale is a Baptist minister living in Teddington, west London. He has written books on preaching and communication for St Andrew Press and is a regular contributor to *Pause for Thought* on BBC Radio 2. He is a tutor with the College of Preachers and blogs at richardlittledale.me.uk.

Peter Hatton is a Methodist minister serving as a tutor at Bristol Baptist College, which trains people from many different streams of church for varied ministries in the UK. He is passionate about the importance for Christians of reclaiming the practical wisdom of scripture.

Paula Gooder is Theologian in Residence for the Bible Society. Her specialism is St Paul, particularly 2 Corinthians, but she has a strong and abiding love for the Gospels—especially the Gospel of Mark. She lives in Birmingham with her husband and two daughters.

David Firth is an Australian Baptist minister who teaches Old Testament at St John's College, Nottingham. He is married and has three adult children.

Joanne Cox-Darling is a Methodist presbyter in Westminster, and the Regional Coordinator for London in the Methodist Church. She is the chair of the Christian Enquiries Agency.

Steve Walton is a researcher and teacher in New Testament and an Anglican priest. He is Professorial Research Fellow at St Mary's University, Twickenham, and Honorary Research Fellow at Tyndale House, Cambridge. Steve is presently working on a major commentary on Acts.

Ian Macnair worked in church pastoral ministry, Bible college lecturing and administration before his retirement. His writings include *Teach Yourself New Testament Greek* (Nelson, 1995).

Richard Briggs is Lecturer in Old Testament and Director of Biblical Studies at Cranmer Hall, St John's College, Durham. He has written widely on biblical interpretation, including *Reading the Bible Wisely: An introduction to taking Scripture seriously* (Cascade Books, 2011).

Watcyn James is a minister in the Presbyterian Church of Wales. At present he is engaged in rural evangelism, training a new generation of preachers and preaching extensively throughout Wales.

The Editor writes...

What attracts you about the summer months? If you are a teacher, it could be the thought of seven weeks away from the classroom. For a parent of young children, those same seven weeks might seem rather a challenge! If you are keen on cricket, it may be the thought of exciting Test matches; for others, the dream of relaxing on a beach—or something entirely different. Whatever your focus, we hope that the rich and varied materials in *Guidelines* will stimulate you in your Christian discipleship and ministry.

Pentecost is a key festival during these months, and two contributions especially will enrich our thinking about the Holy Spirit. Richard Littledale guides us through some insights about the Holy Spirit from Paul's letter to the Romans, while Steve Walton, writing on Acts 8—16, unwraps some of the ways in which the Holy Spirit was at work in the life of the expanding church as it faced new contexts and issues.

Joanne Cox-Darling uses key texts from both Old and New Testaments to help us with the challenges of developing leaders in a missional context: 'Leadership... demands creativity, hospitality, spiritual anointing, timeliness, vision and courage.'

Our Old Testament study includes four fascinating but very different books. Ezekiel is often considered one of the strangest prophets, but Paul Moore's carefully selected passages, together with his thoughtful comments, provide a valuable way of engaging with this material. Peter Hatton is one of a growing number of scholars who are re-evaluating the significance of Wisdom material for shaping contemporary discipleship. His writing on Proverbs is thus most envigorating. David Firth's exploration of Esther shows how it speaks to our postmodern context in surprising ways. Finally, if you think of Daniel as the most perplexing prophetic book, Richard Briggs comes to your rescue as he takes us skilfully through this text.

Undergirding all of this are Paula Gooder's three weeks of notes on Mark 8—12, linking to the 2015 lectionary Gospel. She illuminates these familiar chapters with fresh insights, enabling us to reconnect with Jesus. And there is more. Ian Macnair's study of 1 Timothy provides us with early church approaches to many aspects of contemporary Christian life, while Watcyn James brings his pastoral heart and brain to bear on Paul's letter to the Philippians.

Please enjoy the summer months accompanied by the riches of these amazing Scriptures.

David Spriggs

The BRF Prayer

Almighty God,
you have taught us that your word is a lamp for our
feet and a light for our path. Help us, and all who
prayerfully read your word, to deepen our
fellowship with you and with each other through your love.
And in so doing may we come to know you more fully,
love you more truly, and follow more faithfully in
the steps of your son Jesus Christ, who lives and
reigns with you and the Holy Spirit,
one God for evermore. Amen.

Ezekiel

Ezekiel introduces himself to us on his 30th birthday in 593BC (1:1–3). He is standing by a canal some 50 miles south of Baghdad, in what is now Iraq. On that very day, as the son of a priest, Ezekiel should have been about 900 miles away in the temple in Jerusalem, beginning his first day as a fully qualified priest, a role he had been preparing for since childhood.

Five years previously, though, when Ezekiel was 25 years old and able to start his apprenticeship training in the temple, everything had gone wrong. Judah's king, Jehoiachin, rebelled against King Nebuchadnezzar of Babylon, who sent his armies to lay siege to Jerusalem. They ransacked the city and Jehoiachin and all the leading citizens were deported to Babylon (2 Kings 24:10–16). Ezekiel and his wife were among several thousand people forced to eke out a living as best they could in exile. His priestly career was over before it had begun.

The whole experience was deeply traumatic and confusing for Ezekiel and the exiles. Psalm 137 expresses their feelings of bitter loss, grief and anger. It was a severe blow to their faith in the Lord their God. They had believed that God was committed to defending his people and his holy city from their enemies, and we see this faith confidently expressed, for example, in Psalms 46 and 48. They now felt that the Lord had either abandoned them or been shamefully defeated by the gods of Babylon. His name and his people had been made a mockery.

As we shall see, however, God had not finished with his people yet. After five years of exile, the Lord sprang a birthday surprise on Ezekiel.

Quotations are taken from the New International Version of the Bible unless otherwise stated.

4–10 May

1 'I saw visions of God'

Ezekiel 1:4—2:1

What seems to be a storm cloud approaching (v. 4) turns out to be a life-changing revelation of God. Ezekiel struggles to describe the indescribable, using the Hebrew word for 'something like' 18 times. Rather than analysing the vision, we do well to enter into Ezekiel's intense experience and feel something of his breathless awe.

As the bright, flashing cloud draws near, Ezekiel sees four strange winged creatures, each with four faces (vv. 5–14). He would have seen statues and pictures of beings like these in Babylon, usually supporting a god's throne or guarding a temple or the king's palace. They denote the presence of deity. What strikes Ezekiel about them is that they can move in any direction without turning (v. 9), because of their wheels within wheels, which are powered by the spirit of the deity (vv. 15–21).

As Ezekiel looks up, he sees a transparent dome over the creatures' heads, separating the throne of a holy, transcendent God from the world (v. 26), and seated on this bright blue throne is a fiery human-like figure wrapped in a rainbow (vv. 27–28). At the climax of the vision, Ezekiel realises what he is seeing: it is not one of the gods of Babylon but a glimpse of the glory of Yahweh, the Lord God of Israel. This is the God whom Ezekiel was born to serve, whose throne is in the midst of his people in the temple in Jerusalem—except that his chariot-throne can go anywhere and is now right here by the Chebar canal with the exiles. Their God has not been defeated; he is still on his throne. He has not abandoned them; he is present in Babylon in all his power and glory to speak to this mere mortal, a redundant priest.

Like others in scripture who are privileged to see the glory of the Lord (see Revelation 1:13–17), Ezekiel falls flat on his face in submission. The Lord commands him to stand and God's Spirit sets him on his feet, enabling him to listen and receive his commission.

2 'I am sending you to a nation of rebels'

Ezekiel 2:3—3:17

The Lord tells Ezekiel of his new role as God's messenger to the people of Israel. Unlike others whom he calls to be prophets, such as Moses, Samuel and Jeremiah (Exodus 3:4; 1 Samuel 3; Jeremiah 1:11), the Lord never calls Ezekiel by name. This prophet is always addressed as 'son of man', a mere mortal, called to serve his creator. Ezekiel, in effect, loses his life in God's service (see Mark 8:35), as 'the hand of the Lord' takes hold of him, taking away his ability to speak for long periods (3:25–27), lifting him and moving him from place to place, sometimes literally and sometimes in visions (3:14; 8:3).

God is sending Ezekiel to a people who, for generations, have rebelled against God as their protector and ruler (2:3–4). He will face inevitable pain and danger but must fearlessly speak God's message, so that, whether or not they pay attention, 'they will know that a prophet has been among them' (v. 5). This is the first appearance of a key phrase, 'they will know', which is repeated with variants some 78 times in the course of the book. This 'recognition refrain' is rather like a musical motif or theme. It reminds us of the Lord's purpose and plan, that mortals should come to recognise how he has acted in sovereign power as ruler and judge of all. In the present context, the Lord is determined that the exiles will come to recognise that God has sent them his prophet.

This prophet must not be rebellious (v. 8). He must obediently eat and digest a seemingly unpalatable message of judgement, so that it becomes part of him (2:8—3:2). Ezekiel is surprised by its sweetness (3:3), which is perhaps a hint of the blessing that comes from receiving even the hardest truths from God's word (see Psalm 19:7–11).

Ezekiel's heavy responsibility is to be a watchman for Israel, giving the exiles early warning of approaching disaster (v. 17). They will not listen, because they have hard heads and stubborn hearts (v. 7), but God has made his prophet just as unyielding, lest he give way to fear or dismay (vv. 8–9). There is a certain irony in this, because Ezekiel's name means 'God strengthens', but his encounter with God leaves him utterly exhausted for a week (v. 15).

3 Prophet of doom

Ezekiel 4:1–7; 5:1–13

Ezekiel begins his prophetic ministry to the exiles by spending over a year performing a silent one-man drama. We can imagine quite a crowd gathering at 'show time' to watch and heckle his strange repeated antics and to speculate on their meaning as the months go by.

First, Ezekiel is told to act the part of the enemy besieging Jerusalem, the city to which the exiles longed to return. In mime he must show that the

Lord is against his people, his face set against their city, his arm bared in judgement (4:1–3, 7; see Isaiah 52:10). Then Ezekiel must lie on his side as if a guilty prisoner, bound and lying in a cell (v. 4). Presumably he did this only for part of each day, because he also had to weigh and prepare his rations (vv. 9–12). The trouble coming upon the city is portrayed as the Lord's punishment for over four centuries of sin (vv. 5–6).

When suddenly, one day, Ezekiel whips out a sword and begins to shave off his hair and beard, it must bring people running to see this dangerous new charade (5:1). Priests were forbidden to shave their heads and beards (Leviticus 21:5), so this is an extraordinary act of self-humiliation, depicting the fate of the city's population (v. 12).

Now Ezekiel's tongue is loosed for the first time to speak God's message of doom. The sin of the city is described: set like a jewel among the nations, she has turned out to be a carbuncle, worse than the surrounding nations, rejecting the way of life commanded by the Lord God who dwells there among his people, and preferring the ways of the other nations. So God is coming against her in judgement, bringing disaster (vv. 5–12).

At this point, the 'recognition refrain' that we first saw in 2:5 appears again (5:13), and it is repeated three more times in the following chapter (6:7, 10, 14) in connection with the terrible punishments that will fall on God's people because of their idolatry. The unrelentingly doom-laden message is that disaster is coming (7:5), and when the punishments fall, this rebel nation will recognise that the Lord, their holy judge, has kept his word.

4 Leaving home

Ezekiel 8:1–4, 16–18; 9:1–7; 11:5–25

In chapters 8—11, Ezekiel recounts a second visionary experience some 14 months after his first vision of God's glory (8:1). The human-like figure seen in 1:26 lifts the prophet by his hair and, in a nightmarish vision, takes him to where the exiles longed to be—home in Jerusalem. All is not well here, however. In the temple, where Ezekiel would have served as a priest, he is shown blatant idolatry. Men are worshipping the sun in the inner court of the Lord's house, the palace (the Hebrew word *hekal* means both 'temple' and 'palace') where the people's true king dwelt among his people (8:16).

God pronounces that he must 'deal with them in anger' (v. 18) and calls avenging angels to 'begin at my sanctuary' (9:6) and slaughter the guilty, even though their bodies will further defile God's house. In the next chapter, burning coals from God's fiery throne are to be cast upon the city (10:2). Then the Lord's glorious throne rises up and moves eastwards. The unthinkable is about to happen: the Lord is abandoning his sanctuary (10:18). The message of judgement ends with the 'recognition refrain', 'And you will know that I am the Lord' (11:12).

Horrified, Ezekiel falls face down and cries out in anguish to the Lord (v. 13). In the moment of crisis, a word of mercy and hope is given to this prophet of doom, almost the only relief from his relentless message of judgement. Although God is leaving his sanctuary, his holy place, he himself has been 'a sanctuary' to the exiles. He plans eventually to bring them home and give them a new heart and an obedient spirit to enable them to be God's people again (vv. 17—20).

Ezekiel watches as the glory of the Lord, which had filled the temple built by Solomon 365 years before, finally departs (v. 23; 1 Kings 8:11). The vision ends and the watchman finds himself back with the exiles. Now, whether or not they listen, he must relive the horror as he tells them what he has been shown.

5 Grim tales

Ezekiel 16:1–22, 34–38, 60–63

In addition to mimed and spoken prophecies, the word of the Lord came to Ezekiel in the form of parables or allegories. Chapters 15—17 contain three examples. In the first, Jerusalem is likened to a fruitless vine, fit only for firewood (ch. 15). The third is like a political cartoon, depicting Judah's disastrous hope of making Egypt her ally and protector (17:1–21).

The second and much longer parable, in chapter 16, is a bitter, twisted version of a rags-to-riches folk tale in which a foundling child is gallantly rescued by a prince and grows up to become his queen. The twist is that this couple do not live happily ever after, because Queen Jerusalem (representing the whole nation) is a promiscuous slut who shows neither love nor gratitude to her husband and benefactor. She forgets how he saved her when she was naked and helpless. She squanders on her lovers the gifts with which he beautified her and the food that he provided for her (vv. 17–19). She is worse than a prostitute, because she pays her lovers (v. 34).

Previous prophets, such as Hosea and Jeremiah, likened Israel's worship of idols to marital infidelity (Hosea 1:2; Jeremiah 3:1–2). Ezekiel's tale (along with the related story of two sisters in chapter 23) is far more shocking and disturbing, even today, despite the fact that most translations tone down the crudity of the imagery and language found in the original. The Lord uses shock tactics to try to make the exiles sit up and listen to the reason why they have ended up in Babylon and why there is still more punishment to come. Far from home and longing to return to all they hold most dear, the exiles must be appalled by this horrible revision of their nation's history. The princess whose beauty once displayed her Lord's splendour before the nations will be stripped and humiliated (16:14, 37–38).

After such a diatribe, the promises in the last three verses (vv. 61–63) come as a surprise. Jerusalem may forget, but God will remember his covenant and forgive all that she has done. Then she will recognise her true love.

6 Sin and sour grapes

Ezekiel 18

The proverb with which this chapter begins (v. 2) was in common use among the exiles and was also familiar back home in Jerusalem (Jeremiah 31:29). It reveals how the exiles viewed their troubles. The conjunction between the two halves of the proverb could be translated as either 'and' or 'but'. If we use 'and', then the tone of the saying is fatalistic. This is just how life is: 'We are simply paying the price, picking up the debt for the sins of previous generations. There's nothing we can do about it, and it is not our fault.' However, if we use 'but', the proverb becomes a complaint: 'This is unfair; we are innocent victims.' Probably both attitudes were prevalent among the exiles.

The Lord, however, declares the abolition of this proverb and the attitudes it sums up, affirming his ownership of all human lives through all generations (vv. 3–4). His word is that 'the one who sins is the one who will die', the principle upon which the law of Israel was based (see Deuteronomy 24:16). A case study of three generations illustrates this principle

(vv. 5–18). The implication for Ezekiel's hearers is that they are yet another sinful generation, and so cannot shift the blame or complain of injustice.

More urgently and importantly, the Lord not only judges each person justly but also takes no pleasure in condemning the wicked. Rather, he delights in giving sinners the opportunity to repent and receive forgiveness. Those who turn back to God and change their ways will not have their previous sins counted against them; they will live (vv. 21–24). But previous good deeds will be of no help to those who turn to the bad, either. What counts is the direction they are facing now. How sins can be taken away is not explained here, nor how people can possibly acquire the new heart and spirit they need in order to change their behaviour (see 11:19; 36:26). God simply presses home his gospel appeal, pleading with the exiles to repent and live (vv. 31–32).

Guidelines

Ezekiel's visions and prophecies to the exiles continue to have relevance for us today. Various aspects of his prophecies are picked up within the New Testament. Those who believe in Christ are described as 'exiles' (1 Peter 1:1) whose 'citizenship is in heaven' (Philippians 3:20). Elements of Ezekiel's first overwhelming encounter with God reappear in John's vision of the exalted Lord Jesus Christ and his description of God's throne (Revelation 1:12–17; 4:2–8).

How might reflection on Ezekiel's vision deepen our spirituality? Ezekiel shows us the glory of the Lord our God. He is Lord over all creation, not limited to a single place or nationality. He is all-powerful and undefeated and never abandons his people or purposes. He is the perfectly holy and just judge of all. He abhors our ungrateful rebellion and infidelity to the love he has shown us, yet he takes no pleasure in condemning the wicked.

Ezekiel saw the glory of God in 'something that seemed like a human form' (1:26, NRSV). It is in the face of Jesus Christ, the 'Son of Man', the Word made flesh, who lived, died, rose again and reigns over all for ever, that 'we have seen his glory' (John 1:14; 2 Corinthians 4:6). God has come to us, a world in exile, not to condemn but save us (John 3:16–17). In his grace and mercy, he warns and urges us to take his escape route from death to life, making it possible for sinners to repent and make a new start.

1 'For the sake of my name'

Ezekiel 20:1–44

About a year after Ezekiel's vision of the glory of the Lord leaving the temple, God gives the exiles a history lesson. The surprise in this new account of the story of God's dealings with Israel is that God's people were rebels even back in Egypt. God chose them and promised to lead them to a land of plenty (vv. 5–6), but they would not give up the religious practices of Egypt (vv. 7–8). God did not pour out his anger on them there in Egypt because of his concern for his reputation among the surrounding nations (vv. 8–9).

History repeats itself. God leads his people out of Egypt into the wilderness, where they reject his laws (vv. 9–13), but, for the sake of his name, he does not destroy them (vv. 14–17). The next generation is no better but is spared for the same reason (vv. 18–22). The people God brings into the land continue to be rebels (v. 28). Every generation has gone astray, and the present generation is no exception (vv. 30–31), demonstrating the principle in chapter 19 that God holds each generation accountable for its own sin.

The phrase 'For the sake of my name' strikes a new note in this chapter. We have noted the recognition refrain 'Then they/you shall know that I am the Lord', which has been used up to this point to express God's purpose when he acts in judgement. The new refrain states why God has repeatedly chosen not to act in judgement but to show mercy. It is not that rebellion can be excused and forgotten. Nor is it out of pity. The reason is that if the Lord were to destroy his people, then the other nations might wonder what kind of weak or faithless God this is who does not fulfil his promises and plans. This was Moses' classic argument for God's mercy in Exodus 32:11–14.

Looking to the future, God reveals to the exiles that he will again show mercy to his people. He will lead them home through another purifying wilderness experience (vv. 33–43). The section concludes by combining both refrains (v. 44) as a promise of the Lord's determination to demonstrate his righteousness by acting in mercy.

2 The cruellest blow

For nearly five years, Ezekiel has been warning the exiles of God's approaching punishment. Now the day of judgement dawns—probably the worst day of his life. Ezekiel is told to record that on this very day, 900 miles away (a journey of six months or more), the king of Babylon has launched his siege against Jerusalem (v. 2). In a final parable, Ezekiel declares that the destruction has begun. The pot is on the fire. After boiling, all the contents will be thrown out and the contaminated pot itself will be consumed by fire (vv. 3–13).

God's prophet must perform one further extraordinary action to mark this day, an action demanding more self-abnegation than anything God has previously required of him. Verses 15–18 are terse but dreadfully moving. This is the first and only mention of Ezekiel's wife, and within a couple of sentences she is dead. Not only does the Lord take away his most precious companion but he forbids Ezekiel to mourn. Ezekiel obeys without a murmur of complaint, showing how utterly dedicated he has become as the Lord's servant (v. 18; compare 4:14). His wife meant everything to him, but he will tell us nothing about her.

Ezekiel's strange refusal to mourn is meant to provoke the exiles to ask, 'Why?' (v. 19), so that Ezekiel can tell them that their greatest treasure and delight, Jerusalem, the focus of all their hopes, will also be taken away (v. 21). One day, a messenger will arrive in Babylon with terrible news of the siege and fall of the city, proving that Ezekiel's prophecies were from God. Then the exiles will not mourn. Instead they will be consumed with shame as they finally recognise the hand of God in these events.

God's action in this chapter provokes us too to ask, 'Why?' How could a God of love put his messenger through such an ordeal? One response from our New Testament perspective is that God never asks of his servants any greater sacrifice than that which God himself made in giving up his beloved Son to die on the cross. Poor Ezekiel and his wife were caught up in the great story of the loving purposes of God, a story that ultimately would lead to victory over sin and death through the suffering of another obedient servant.

3 The moment of truth

Ezekiel 33

The story of Ezekiel and the exiles comes to a suspense-filled pause at the end of chapter 24. The bereaved prophet sits alone, unable to speak (see 24:27), while the exiles anxiously await news that might confirm or deny Ezekiel's awful prediction of Jerusalem's fall.

A sense of time passing is given by the interpolation at this point of Ezekiel's prophecies against seven other nations (Ammon, Moab, Edom, Philistia, Tyre, Sidon and Egypt). As judge of all, God condemns the malice they have shown towards Israel, and the arrogance of their kings (chs. 26—32).

Then, two years later, a ragged, wasted figure stumbles into Ezekiel's house, the first escapee to make the six-month journey bearing the dreaded news that Jerusalem has fallen (33:21). The moment of truth has arrived for the exiles. Ezekiel has been vindicated: his prediction was correct. The exiles now know that he is a true prophet who speaks God's truth (see 2:5; Deuteronomy 18:22).

On this day of bad news, Ezekiel's calling to be a watchman for the exiles is renewed. If his warning is heeded, lives can be saved (vv. 2–5; see 3:17–21). There seems to be a new attitude among the exiles. They recognise that Ezekiel has been speaking the truth about their rebellious wickedness and acknowledge that they are now wasting away under the shameful weight of their sin, just as Ezekiel said they would (v. 10; 24:23). So God renews his plea to them to repent so that a fresh start might be possible (vv. 11–16; previously heard in 18:27–30).

The chapter ends on a darker note with two warnings. The first is against false hope (vv. 23–29). The few poor people left behind in the promised land must not assume it has been gifted to them, for they too are idolaters under judgement. How God might possibly restore his people is yet to be revealed.

The second warning (vv. 30–33) is for Ezekiel himself, who now finds himself fêted like the winner of a TV singing contest. He must not assume that popularity equals success. The exiles eagerly listen to God's word but still do not act on it.

4 'Can these bones live?'

Ezekiel's third vision begins with horror but ends with hope. The Spirit of God sets him down on the site of what appears to be a catastrophic battle—a lifeless, silent scene of massacre or genocide, a grisly memorial with bones picked clean by vultures and wild beasts (vv. 1–2). To Ezekiel the priest, this is an accursed, unclean place, but God forces him to walk among the bones and inspect the hopeless desolation. This is how the exiles feel now that they recognise that the judgement of God has fallen on them because of their rebellion (v. 11). They feel defeated, finished, without hope.

God asks, 'Can these bones live?' (v. 3). The exiles would say, 'No, of course not!' but Ezekiel's answer shows submissive faith. He believes that God has power and authority to do this extraordinary thing, yet he does not presume on God to do it.

By commanding Ezekiel to prophesy to the bones (vv. 4–6), the Lord authorises his prophet of doom to become a prophet of hope for the rebirth of the nation. The recognition refrain, 'You shall know that I am the Lord', is no longer a threat of death but has become a promise of new life.

Through his word God reveals his promises and plans to his people, and by his Spirit he acts to fulfil his word. Ezekiel, grasped by the Spirit, obediently proclaims God's message, and the miracle begins as the bones come together and are covered with sinews and flesh (vv. 7–8). Then he must call for the breath of God to give these corpses the kiss of life (v. 10). This two-stage rebirth echoes God's creation of Adam in Genesis 2:7, but it is like resurrection from the grave for the exiles (v. 13).

Ezekiel's vision illustrates God's plan to give a new heart and his Spirit to his people to enable them to live holy lives (36:26–27), to raise sinners from the horror of death to the living hope of resurrection life (1 Peter 1:3).

5 The last battle

We need to bear in mind that these later chapters of Ezekiel are still addressed to exiles, far from their home city, which they now know lies in ruins. They have begun to recognise current events as God's just punishment for rebellion, and the Lord has revealed to Ezekiel his future plan to resurrect the nation and bring the people back to their land.

At this point we might be tempted to skip straight to Ezekiel's final vision of that glorious future restoration, because the strange prophecy in chapters 38—39 seems to interrupt the flow. It envisages a utopian future when God's people are once again living peacefully in the land without any need for protective fortifications (38:11). Gog, a mysterious evil prince, will lead a vast alliance of armies in a malicious, unprovoked attack on Israel (38:14–16), but the Lord God will utterly defeat them before they can strike the first blow (39:3–4). The corpses of Gog's vast army will provide a seven-year feast for birds and beasts (vv. 4, 17–20), their weapons will keep the towns stocked with firewood for seven years (v. 9) and their burial will take seven months (v. 12). The number seven symbolises perfection and completeness, so, in other words, all evil will be utterly expunged and peace will be eternally won.

This is, of course, an idealised eschatological depiction of a final battle between God and the massed forces of evil, which is reworked in Revelation 19:11—20:15. Both these prophecies are 'apocalyptic': that is, they are revelatory (the Greek word *apocalupsis* means 'uncovering', the lifting of a veil to show a truth or disclose knowledge). This 'last battle' will reveal God's true sovereignty, power and glory. Israel will recognise the glory of the Lord when they see his victory and reflect on how he has acted in judgement and mercy towards his people (vv. 22, 28). The nations will recognise God's justice meted out to them and his holiness in his dealings with Israel (vv. 21, 27). For the exiles still far from home and awaiting liberation, there is an assurance that ultimately the Lord our God will be victorious over all evil, the old order of things will have passed away, and his people will live in peace with him for ever (v. 29; Revelation 21:3–4).

6 Land of hope and glory

Ezekiel 40:1–4; 43:1–12; 47:1–12; 48:35

It is New Year's Day in the 25th year of the exile when the hand of the Lord transports Ezekiel to his homeland once again in a final visionary journey. All that the prophet observes is to be faithfully reported back as his final word to the exiles, a message of new hope for the future (40:4). It is exactly 14 years since Jerusalem was reduced to rubble, but Ezekiel is given a guided tour of a new city complex, perfectly designed for God and his people to dwell in together.

We tend to find all the measurements and detailed description of the new temple somewhat tedious, but we need to remember that Ezekiel was a frustrated priest and he would have been thrilled by every detail. This is a dream temple, in contrast to the nightmare temple of chapter 8, which was full of abominable idolatry. It is rather like an architect's computer model through which you can take a virtual tour. This new improved temple atop the mountain is a holy sanctuary fit for the Lord, set apart from the city and the king's palace, carefully designed and regulated to ensure that the holy and the common elements are kept separate and all the correct sacrifices are offered continually on behalf of God's people (43:7–9, 12, 18–27; 44:15–19). Ezekiel, who back in 10:18 and 11:22–23 saw God abandon his defiled temple and city, now falls face down as God's glory returns to his temple for ever more (43:1–5).

Ezekiel's vision is a perfect model of life in the kingdom of God. All shall be well now that 'The Lord is There' (48:35). As Ezekiel paddles, wades and then swims in the great river flowing out from the temple, he observes how the Lord's holy presence at the heart of the city and land leads to abundant blessing (47:1–12). The river brings new life everywhere it flows, transforming the Dead Sea so that it teems with fish and creating a new Eden full of constantly fruiting trees whose leaves have special healing properties.

This is a vision of the perfect new life that God promised to the exiles (37:26–27), but they had another 35 years to wait before they would be allowed to make the long journey home, and when they got there it was to find Jerusalem and the temple still in ruins. Another 23 years passed before a new temple was completed, but it seemed pathetic compared with the glory of Solomon's temple (Haggai 2:3). Was Ezekiel's final glorious vision simply an unattainable dream?

Guidelines

Imagine Jerusalem, centuries later, bustling with pilgrims celebrating the harvest festival of Tabernacles. For six days a golden flagon has been filled with water from the Pool of Siloam and carried in procession to the temple to be poured out in thanksgiving to God. On the final and greatest day of the feast a man in the crowd suddenly shouts out, 'Let anyone who is thirsty come to me and drink. Whoever believes in me… rivers of living water will flow from within them' (John 7:37–38).

This is the fulfilment of Ezekiel's final vision. In Jesus Christ we see the glory of the Lord (John 1:14). Jesus is the temple that will be destroyed and rebuilt (John 2:19–21). His death and resurrection bring us rebirth through the Holy Spirit (John 3:5), and from him flows fullness of life, healing and peace.

The epistle to the Hebrews (possibly written for disciples from a priestly background) explains how Jesus is our great high priest, the mediator of the new covenant that Ezekiel proclaimed, whose sacrificial offering of himself fulfilled for ever the temple system for dealing with the sin that prevents us from living in relationship with God (Hebrews 9:10–18).

This is why, in the final vision of the new Jerusalem in Revelation, there is no longer any need for a temple with holy areas. The presence and glory of the Lord God and the Lamb now fill the whole city (Revelation 21:22–23) and the life-giving river flows, bringing life and blessing to God's kingdom (22:1–2).

Ezekiel probably died in exile and never returned to Jerusalem (he would have been 84 years old by the time the exiles were allowed to go home). With his priestly background and training, we can imagine him being shocked by the way the New Testament recycles his visions and prophecies. Perhaps, though, his eyes might fill with tears of recognition and joy as he reads about a prophet who suffered rejection by his own people and died for a lost and rebellious world, an obedient priest who offered himself as the one perfect sacrifice for the sins of the whole world—the Lord Jesus Christ, the resurrection and the life.

FURTHER READING

Christopher J.H. Wright, *The Message of Ezekiel*, IVP, 2001.

The Holy Spirit in Romans

Many regard Paul as a 'man of letters'. With his Jewish pedigree, his rabbinical training and his schooling at the university of Tarsus, he was certainly that: he makes no secret of it when he describes himself as a 'Hebrew of Hebrews' in Philippians 3:4–6. Furthermore, some of the most tightly argued passages anywhere in the New Testament are found in the letter to the Romans. In the pages of this letter, Paul deals with weighty matters of law, grace, Jewish heritage and imputed righteousness, to name but some—but is there any room for the Holy Spirit among all that theological argument? In fact, right from the start, Paul makes it clear that his answer is 'yes'. Before the first (very long) sentence of the letter is complete, Paul has acknowledged the role of the Holy Spirit in the resurrection of Jesus, who 'through the Spirit of holiness was appointed the Son of God in power' (Romans 1:4). He goes on to describe the Holy Spirit's integral role in every aspect of the Christian's life, both individual and corporate. Christianity without the Holy Spirit is as inconceivable as a balloon without air or a bird without wings.

This week, we shall look at six different roles of the Holy Spirit as described by Paul in Romans. As is often the case in the New Testament, the Spirit is described more in terms of function than in terms of character. I have called these functions of the Spirit 'hallmark', 'compass', 'guarantor', 'interpreter', 'engineer' and 'glue'. You won't find Paul using those six words, but we shall see him describing those six functions. The list is not exhaustive, and you will find other mentions of the Holy Spirit in Romans, as well as the references chosen here. As you work through these different passages, you may find that there are other descriptions that work better for you to describe the work of the Holy Spirit.

As a young man I always wanted to make a big impact for God, and a wise Christian friend gave me this advice: 'Richard—it's not about you having a monopoly on the Holy Spirit, but the Holy Spirit having a monopoly on you.' Sound advice indeed!

Unless otherwise stated, quotations are from the New International Version of the Bible.

1 The Spirit as hallmark

Romans 2:25–29

We often use the phrase 'in spirit' as a substitute for 'not really', as in, for example, 'I'll be there *in spirit*'. To Paul's fellow Jews, he was a heretic who had gone soft on the demands of the law in his pursuit of Christ. They believed that he had sold out and brought shame on the faith of his fathers. Here he explains that nothing could be further from the truth.

For centuries past, circumcision had been a badge of honour to the Jewish male, declaring his place among the chosen people, but Paul dares to question whether that is really what makes him a Jew: 'A person is not a Jew who is one only outwardly' (v. 28). He goes on to say that what matters is a 'circumcision of the heart' (v. 29). Such talk falls very awkwardly on our Western ears. However, despite the embarrassment it causes, the point stands in any age and any culture. The 'trappings' of Christianity, whether it be a sticker on the car, a badge in our lapel, a Bible tucked under our arm or even the habit of churchgoing, are not the heart of the matter. It is the attitude of the heart, rather than any physical sign, that truly marks us out as God's people.

We might even say that obeying the demands of a Spirit who resides within is harder than keeping rules that exist outside. Inner attitudes never stay hidden for long: as Jesus said of false prophets, 'by their fruit you will recognise them' (Matthew 7:16). If we truly have a relationship with the Spirit of God, it means that he will coax, nudge and prompt us to behave like God's people. When we do those things, we end up as much a part of God's people as anyone who bears a physical mark of recognition (v. 26), and maybe even more so (v. 27). When that happens, the presence of the Spirit to guide us and prompt our righteous actions serves as a hallmark of our membership in the family of God.

Each of us must decide every day whether our life will be lived by the internal nudge of the Spirit or by the external influences of the world, even the 'Christian' world. Do we bear the hallmark of God's presence today?

2 The Spirit as inner compass

Romans 7:4–11, 21–23; 8:5–6

Over the years, many people have argued about whether the person Paul describes in Romans 7 is a Christian or not. Some have said that the internal struggle he describes in verses 7–11 could not possibly describe a Christian and that Paul is outlining a life without grace, contrasting it with a grace-filled life in chapter 8. Personally, I have no doubt that Paul is representing the Christian's experience here. I have only to look at my own life, with its catalogue of mistakes and its tapestry of faith and doubt, to know that it is me he is talking about. Who has not felt the titanic struggle that Paul describes in verses 21–23, in which we see the good choice and end up doing the opposite?

Philosophers from ancient times to the present day have wrestled with our capacity to recognise good while doing evil. In the midst of that struggle, the Holy Spirit can act as our internal compass to point us in God's direction. He ushers us into what Paul describes as the 'new way of the Spirit' (7:6). Long before the days of satnav, my father always used to drive with a 'floating' compass fixed to the dashboard. There would be no point in my doing the same because I quite simply wouldn't take any notice of it! If we want to head in God's direction, then we have to make a conscious effort to abide by the guidance he gives us.

Paul describes us in Romans 8:5 as those who 'have their minds set on what the Spirit desires'. Of course, this is not a once-and-for-all setting. The decision to follow the needle of the Spirit's compass involves not one but 1001 choices. They might include everything from how we fill our day to the books we read and the things on which we spend our money. Through the Holy Spirit, God provides a completely reliable compass to guide us in his way. The only unreliable element is ourselves, which is why we must make a daily effort to take more and more notice of the Spirit. Packing a compass for your journey is one thing, but heeding it is another.

3 The Spirit as guarantor

Romans 8:9–17

Some years ago, I had to sign a legal document to act as guarantor for my son. My signature stood as a guarantee that he was who he said he was, and that should he ever default on his rental payments, I would step in for him.

Every once in a while, even the strongest Christian is plagued by doubts. We doubt our forgiveness, we are uncertain about our destiny, and even our identity as sons and daughters of God seems doubtful. Paul himself knew what it was like to feel discouraged and came close to giving up when he was working in Corinth. (You can read the story in Acts 18:1–11.) At such times, we need a guarantor—some kind of reassurance that, however we may feel, we still belong to God. In Romans 8, Paul describes the Spirit in just such a way. So long as the Spirit lives within us (v. 9), we are never without a witness to God's presence in our lives. Even when our bodies start to wear out through age and infirmity, he is still there, like an inextinguishable flame burning within (v. 11). As a pastor it has been my privilege to attend many people at their deathbed and I have seen this time and time again—the resurrection power of Jesus showing through our human weakness by the presence of the Spirit.

Of course, none of us is a natural child of God: we are all adopted (v. 15). As much as we might believe that to be the case, the Spirit helps us to feel it, enables us to cry out to God as a child does to a father. 'By him we cry, "Abba, Father"' writes Paul, using an intimate word akin to 'daddy' or 'papa'.

Once again, though, as we have seen in previous passages, the activity of the Spirit is consensual. Six times in this short passage Paul uses the word 'if'. The Spirit may nudge, prompt and guide, but he will never force us to act. If we want to live in 'the realm of the Spirit' (v. 9) and to sense our identity as sons and daughters of God deep within, we must abide by his guidance and heed his promptings.

4 The Spirit as interpreter

Romans 8:19–27

Think of the Old Testament story of the tower of Babel (Genesis 11:1–9), an account of a foolish attempt to fly in the face of God, and the confusion of languages that resulted from it. Those arrogant architects have a lot to answer for—not least, the years I spent sweating over vocabulary books in French and German! Sometimes, though, even when we speak the same tongue, it doesn't feel like the same language, as many a teenager and his or her parents would testify.

It often feels as if we and God don't speak the same language. After all, we live in time and he dwells in eternity. We are bound by the limitations of a body that is ageing and a planet that is decaying, while he remains for ever unchanged. It is not just the new Christian who says, 'I don't know what to pray for', but sometimes the more experienced Christian, too. Because the Spirit is a person of the Trinity and therefore one with God, but also dwells within every Christian, he is in a unique position to help us. With unusual candour, Paul describes the Christian's dilemma when we 'do not know what we ought to pray for' (v. 26). The Spirit comes to our aid as a kind of interpreter, giving us an insight into how to pray (v. 27).

Note that sometimes the Spirit's help may result in prayers which are so heartfelt and profound that they are sub-linguistic, coming out as groans or sighs (v. 26). This may or may not be the same experience as praying in tongues. What is certain, though, is that a prayer that comes out as the sigh of exasperation or the puff of defeat may be the most genuine prayer of all. As the psalmist wrote centuries ago, 'Before a word is on my tongue, you, Lord, know it completely' (Psalm 139:4).

Years ago, I was working on a mission team in Belgium, constantly switching between French and English. Sometimes, when it came to praying, my brain felt like such a linguistic mush that groans were just about the only prayer I could manage. I like to think that, at those times, the Spirit acted as my interpreter.

5 The Spirit as engineer

Romans 12:1–8

My wife's brother-in-law is an engineer. By training and habit, he can look at a design of the structure you want to achieve and work out the practical steps to get you there. A two-dimensional blueprint on a piece of paper makes perfect sense to him, creating at once a three-dimensional model in his head. It's just as well that there are people like him, or no building would ever get built with all the heating ducts and wires in the right places.

Sometimes, when you take a look at the raw material out of which the church is made—people like you and me—you realise that there is a long way to go before we look anything like the kingdom of God. We have petty ambitions, bad habits and very poor memories when it comes to God's promises. Will the church, as a prototype of the kingdom of heaven, ever get built? This is where the Spirit as engineer steps in. In the first instance, he starts to renew our minds (v. 2), working with us as individuals. Then he distributes gifts to left and right, to young and old, as he sees fit, so that the body of the church may function (v. 5).

Some years ago, I attended an international conference at a huge church in America. Over four days we completed a gifts and skills programme that was usually done over four weeks. At the end of it, we all had a pretty good idea of what gifts the Spirit had distributed to each of us. We were then asked to take up different positions in a circle around the room, according to the gift we had identified. Despite our different ages, traditions and nationalities, the circle was complete—a wonderful picture of the Spirit's role as engineer.

In Romans 12, Paul describes gifts that are different from those listed in 1 Corinthians 12 and 14. Here in Romans, the emphasis is on how we use the gifts we have been given. Paul employs a string of adverbs to make his point: 'generously… diligently… cheerfully'. When it comes to prophesying, he says that it should be 'corresponding to your faith'. In every instance, the particular gift, distributed according to the Spirit's blueprint, should be used as fully as possible. How are you using your gifts today?

6 The Spirit as glue

Romans 14:10–20

It would be easy to read Romans 14 as a bit of a let-down. After all his profound theology about grace, election and adoption, Paul comes back down to earth with a bump by talking about what's on the menu (14:2).

In the first century, it was not uncommon for meat to be 'offered' to an idol in a temple. Since the idol couldn't actually eat it, someone then had to dispose of it, so, in shops near the temple, traders would sell it off. Rather like in the 2013 horsemeat scandal in Britain, shoppers could not be sure where the meat had come from. Some Christians refused to eat meat altogether, just in case it had been offered in idol-worship, and looked down on those who did not share their scruples. To Paul, this ran counter to the very nature of Christian fellowship, since the person who was being judged in this way was no less than a brother or sister in Christ (v. 13).

On one occasion when I was teaching at a Bible college in Serbia, a Serbian friend lent me his mobile for the duration of his visit. Every man's name in his contact book was preceded by the letter B (for brother) and every woman's by the letter S (for sister)—a powerful reminder of the point that Paul is making here. The Spirit is the glue who sticks Christian fellowship together, despite our many differences of age, background, tradition, culture and habit. The kingdom of God, says Paul, is nothing to do with eating and drinking but everything to do with 'righteousness, peace and joy in the Holy Spirit' (v. 17). Driven on by the Spirit, we make every effort to rise above our differences and build each other up (v. 19).

God's Spirit is given that we might see each other differently and strive to maintain the wonderful multicoloured fellowship that he has created. Perhaps we can all think of a fellow Christian whose behaviour makes them very hard for us to love. The things they do and say rub us up so much the wrong way that we would rather avoid them. Perhaps today would be a good day to thank God that the Holy Spirit is as close to them as he is to us.

Guidelines

As Paul prepares to 'sign off' from his friends in Rome, he still wants to tell them about his hopes to visit them, and he also writes a list of endearingly person greetings, which you can read in 16:3–16. Before he gets there, though, he can't help writing what sounds like a closing flourish to the letter: 'May the God of hope fill you with all joy and peace as you trust in him, so that you may overflow with hope by the power of the Holy Spirit' (15:13). We have already seen the Spirit as hallmark, compass, guarantor, interpreter, engineer and glue. I wonder, how would you describe his role here?

FURTHER READING

For an unusual and evocative portrayal of the Holy Spirit, it is worth reading William Paul Young's *The Shack* (Hodder Windblown, 2008).

Proverbs

Proverbs stands in an ancient Middle Eastern tradition that began about 2500 years before Christ, when unknown scribes from Sumer (now southern Iraq) collected hundreds of traditional sayings, ascribing them to the legendary ruler Shuruppak. Writing was new then and it is significant that one of the first uses for this revolutionary art was to record the collective wisdom of the Sumerians.

Like Shuruppak, Proverbs claims to be linked to a wise king, Solomon, who, according to 1 Kings 4:31, 'was wiser than all other men'. However, it is also clear from the text that Solomon is not the author of Proverbs—at least, not as we understand authorship. Not only did 'the men of Hezekiah' bring together a section of the book (Proverbs 25:1) but other voices, such as those of Agur (30:1–33) and Lemuel (31:1–9), sound in it.

Indeed, the scholarly consensus is that Proverbs is a 'collection of collections' at whose heart are the 'proverbs of Solomon' proper (10:1—22:16), 'topped and tailed' by later material. The later material includes the introductory chapters (1—9), which are relatively long poetic meditations and stories, aimed at whetting the reader's appetite for the *meshalim* (the pithy one-liners of the main collection), and other collections and poems that round off the book and complement its teachings. We do not know who gave the book its final shape or exactly when they did so; the best scholarly guess is that they were Judean sages working before the exile (587/6BC) or after the return, some 50 years later.

Be that as it may, Proverbs offers us wisdom, the ability to negotiate the sharp bends in life's journey safely and with some style. It is an intensely practical book, dealing with things often unmentioned in church, such as relationships, work, leadership and conflict. Yet the authors are also convinced that true wisdom comes from God and is intimately connected to the reverent seeking of his ways that it calls the 'fear of the Lord'.

Quotations are taken from the English Standard Version unless otherwise indicated.

1 What is important in life?

Proverbs 1:1–7

One of the most helpful aspects of the book of Proverbs is that, like the Gospels, it begins by telling us what are its central concerns—and they are things of interest to all humanity, not just to believers. Unless the natural desire has been somehow drained or forced out of them, human beings are curious. They seek to know and understand, even (to use a phrase that seems a little strange to many modern ears) to become wise. Moreover, most humans, even though we all live in a world twisted and distorted by sin, have some understanding that fairness, justice and straight dealing make for a flourishing life.

Verses 2–3 offer us qualities of extraordinary value—gifts of the mind that lead to a just, flourishing life. The pace of learning will vary. Some learners, including the naïve and the young (v. 4), will gain something by just starting on the path that leads to wisdom, while the more experienced will be able to go much further (v. 5). Yet the curriculum offered here—the extended poems in the first nine chapters and the pithy one-liners that make up most of the rest of the book—is the same for all. The material often seems simple but, if we reflect upon it carefully, we discover complexities and thought-provoking paradoxes (v. 6). Moreover, a simple explanation is enhanced, not discarded, when a more complex insight is mastered, just as Newtonian mathematics is not totally invalidated by the findings of quantum physics.

Indeed, life presents us with riddles and enigmas, yet Proverbs' deep conviction is that, if we have the right approach, we can grapple with them and make sense of them. The book's term for the underlying attitude that makes true, life-enhancing knowledge possible is 'the fear of the Lord' (v. 7). To fear God is to be in relationship with him and to seek to live in his presence. Like all relationships, this one involves an element of deliberate choice, and there are those who will reject it and the wholesome discipline that comes with it.

2 Ignorance is bliss?

Proverbs 1:8–33

'No one,' said the ancient Greek philosopher Socrates, 'sins willingly.' At first sight, this seems nonsense. Do we not, often enough, wish for, ardently desire and lust after things that are wrong? Socrates' point, however, is that what we want from sin is what we (falsely) believe to be good. The crooked businessman craves financial gain and the thrill of deceiving others; the bully desires the feeling of power and enhanced self-esteem; the idolater longs for the ability to control the powers-that-be in an uncertain world.

It follows that 'sin' is, in essence, a failure to understand what is in our best interests. Jesus' words from the cross, 'Father, forgive them, for they know not what they do' (Luke 23:34), also suggest that sin can arise from ignorance. This is certainly the view of Proverbs here. The violent robbers in verses 11–19 are unaware that their ambush will destroy their own lives as well as the lives of their victims.

Is this an excuse for sin? Can we exculpate ourselves by claiming that we just didn't know what we were doing? By no means, for Proverbs declares that we should have known. Wisdom would have shown us how narrow, self-centred and, indeed, self-destructive is our sinful grasp on what is good, and has been calling out to us, begging us to turn from folly and live. The book pictures the one who calls to us as a woman whose loud cries do not sound in a desert or from an ivory tower but in the busiest places of our communities (vv. 20–21). As Proverbs continues, we will find out more about 'Lady Wisdom' (the form of the word in the original Hebrew suggests that she is an elevated, semi-divine personage). For now, however, the stress falls on her accessibility and her frustrated yearning to come into a relationship with 'the simple'.

What do we think? Can ignorance ever excuse our wrongdoing? Is wisdom really so readily available and such a potent protection against disaster (v. 33)?

3 'The only hereafter is what we're here, after'

Proverbs 3:13–26

The modern economy, we are told, is a 'knowledge economy'. Our success as nations and individuals will depend, so it is said, on acquiring the skills and intellectual competencies that will enable us to outsmart our competitors and stay ahead of the game. This is the reason why 'education, education, education' is vitally important.

Verse 16 might seem to endorse such thinking, for it suggests that wisdom guarantees a long, healthy, wealthy life. However, the verses surrounding this one point away from so simple an understanding. They imply that the real benefits of acquiring wisdom cannot be expressed in monetary terms: to be fully educated is to be, in a very real sense, rich, no matter how full or empty our bank account might be. To be a curious, informed, mature person who is able to assess the opinions and ideas of others in a generous but rigorous way—this is wealth. This is what it means to be truly 'blessed' (v. 13), to have and to hold the 'tree of life' (v. 18). To have our heads crammed with supposedly useful facts and to be trained in marketable skills but to be unacquainted with the rich history of human thought—this is a sort of poverty.

Of course, Proverbs is well aware that a lack of this world's goods is not to be romanticised. Many of its sayings draw attention to the grinding misery that poverty brings (see, for example, 10:15; 13:23; 15:15). Nevertheless, Proverbs 3 offers a truly radical alternative to the ruling ideology of an age that, in the words of Oscar Wilde, 'knows the price of everything and the value of nothing'. If we gain the wisdom celebrated in Proverbs, we shall have aligned ourselves with the very grain of a universe that is profoundly rational because wisdom has been woven into its fabric from the beginning (vv. 19–20).

4 To whom are we listening?

Proverbs 7

If wisdom is such a good thing, why are people not wise? Proverbs' answer is a radical one. Our relationship with wisdom has been undermined by a rival. In our ears sounds another voice beside hers, one so attractive that it can seduce us away from all that will bring us lasting joy and enduring comfort. We have been warned about this deadly enemy of wisdom several times already (2:16–19; 5:1–14; 6:24–26) but in Proverbs 7 she erupts into the book, speaking with her own voice in all her seductive, deceptive power.

She offers a naive young man illicit, adulterous sex (vv. 6–18); she tells him that he will get away with it; that no one will ever know (vv. 19–20). The vivid figurative language of this passage illuminates the way we are tempted to seize short-term pleasures of many kinds without thought to the long-term consequences of our actions, and how we are persuaded to act differently when we are unobserved from when we are in the public eye.

The test of true integrity is what we do when there seems to be no one holding us to account. Asked on a chat show why he had endangered his presidency by his actions with Monica Lewinsky, Bill Clinton replied candidly, 'Because I could.' The gender roles and power dynamics in that sordid affair were very different from those in Proverbs 7, but the principle still stands. The wise, however, know that 'the eyes of the Lord are in every place, keeping watch on the evil and the good' (Proverbs 15:3). They are not deceived into ignoring the truth that actions have consequences—that, indeed, 'you reap whatever you sow' (Galatians 6:7).

The radical message here goes beyond any prudent calculation. It challenges us to ask whose voice we are listening to with love and attention. Is it that of holy Wisdom, kind to humanity, or are our ears attuned to the flattering tones of Folly?

'Solid joys and lasting treasure, none but Zion's children know' (John Newton, in the hymn 'Glorious things of thee are spoken').

5 Playing with God

Proverbs 8:22–36

Wisdom responds in chapter 8. Her refutation of her rival's enticing words repeats her claim that what she offers is of all-surpassing worth (8:1–21), but it goes on to reveal something hinted at before—that her own relationship with God goes back to the very foundation of the world. Wisdom existed before the stuff of which the universe is made; indeed, the rationality she personifies makes the existence of the creation possible. The fact that we live in an ordered, predictable, law-governed cosmos—that somehow the chaos and unpredictability that exist at the sub-atomic level, according to quantum physics, do not prevail at the level of atoms, molecules, planets and galaxies—is down to her.

Compared with this profound, joyful reality, the folly and caprice of sin are unreal, trivial and irrelevant, no matter how attractive it seems and how powerful a grip it can have on the human heart.

There is something else, too: wisdom is not dull. In verse 30 there is a famous difficulty in translation. Wisdom, God's 'delight', playing before him, is described variously as (and here the translators struggle) 'a darling child', 'a master workman', 'a sage counsellor' or even just 'faithfully' (NIV has 'constantly'). Technically, all these renderings are possible. However, I prefer the first option, as it seems more in tune with the language of the rest of verses 30–31. Delight, playfulness and joy: these are the hallmarks of wisdom from the very beginning and for all time—for all time, not just times of relaxation. We dance with holy wisdom in the presence of God when our sports team plays with artistry and flair or when worship discloses God to us in exaltation and in tears. We also share her delight when an engineer discovers an elegant solution to a bridge's problems or when a teacher inspires her class a with desire to learn, when a surgeon concludes a tricky new procedure and the patient survives or when a gardener propagates a new variety.

6 'I will set a feast for them...'

Proverbs 9:1–6

Feasts in the ancient world, as now, were not just about food. They celebrated the events on which human flourishing and well-being are built. When a man and a woman were joined in marriage; when the beginning of a time of peace and plenty, presided over by a beloved monarch, was memorialised; when a life that had blessed the community ended—then people came together to eat, drink and be merry. Of course, such enjoyment can degenerate into licentiousness and vice (see Exodus 32); however, where wisdom presides, this will not happen. Rather, when those who love wisdom respond to her call, they are brought to a place where, as they break bread together, they affirm all that makes for life and learn the arts of sociability.

These words challenge the notion that we can be 'educated' simply by staring at a screen and moving a mouse to choose the right answer in a multiple choice question. A carer can gain a paper qualification in such a way, entitling them to work in a home for elderly people, but where will they learn the compassion that will enable them to treat a confused, angry, vulnerable resident with dignity and respect? Only through social, relational learning, 'offline', can we learn what really matters.

Technology has its place in learning: the written word itself is, after all, an ancient technology. However, the word of God belongs in and to the believing community. There, as it is read, pondered and discussed, Christ comes and opens it to us, just as he did on the road to Emmaus—and our hearts burn within us as the bread is broken. One way of understanding the feast that Wisdom sets before us (v. 2) is to see it as referring to the rich menu of pithy one-line sayings that make up the rest of the book of Proverbs. In spite of the book's ascription to Solomon (1:1), his is not the only hand at work here: the wisdom of Proverbs 10—31 is the wisdom of a whole community. We are called, with many others, to sit down and sample their fare.

Guidelines

- Give thanks for the times when you have acted wisely and justly.
- Ask God to give you the wisdom that will help you in the hard, perplexing times when all your choices seem bad.
- Think about the times when we, individually and collectively, have decided not to know—to turn away from disturbing knowledge, trying to preserve a peace which is no peace.
- 'Solid joys and lasting treasures, none but Zion's children know' (John Newton). What, in your experience, has remained solid and has endured through the years? What now seems flimsy and unsatisfying?
- Ponder the words of the 'Serenity Prayer', ascribed to Reinhold Niebuhr (1892–1971): 'God grant me the serenity to accept the things I cannot change; courage to change the things I can; and wisdom to know the difference.'

- Invite some friends for a meal and delight in their conversation and their wisdom.
- Reflect on the teaching of Jesus and be astonished at its practical, revolutionary wisdom.

1 Wisdom for the day

Proverbs 10:1–14

How do we feast on the rich smorgasbord of pithy one-liners that predominate in the next 21 chapters of Proverbs? One way is to ponder a different saying every day. I have a desk calendar with a proverb for every day, but that kind of assistance isn't necessary. Follow the order as given in the book, occasionally reading two proverbs together and noting where more extended poems occur (for example, in 31:10–31), and your reading will fit, more or less, into a year. If you do savour each saying, it will often, in God's good purposes, match the day's need. However, you don't need to be overly respectful: you may want to question the wisdom offered, comparing it, perhaps, with other proverbs that offer different perspectives (for example, compare verses 4 and 5 of Proverbs 26).

However, for our purposes, a larger sample also has its advantages. Today's selection, Proverbs 10:1–14, has been chosen more or less at random (generally speaking, the arrangement of sayings in the book is not haphazard, but nor is it in accordance with rigid groupings). The advice given in these verses seems, at first sight, to be plain common sense. After all, most of us believe in honest hard work (vv. 2, 4–5) and we know that we can avoid trouble by controlling our mouths (vv. 6, 8, 11, 14). We might also note that two of these seemingly bland commonplaces are very similar to each other (vv. 8, 14). This might seem like carelessness, particularly as people today place such a high value on originality. It is, however, quite deliberate: the sages responsible for Proverbs would have agreed with the 18th-century writer Samuel Johnson that 'people need to be reminded more often than they need to be instructed'.

These sayings may appear to be very plain, but translators sometimes fail to capture their wit. For example, in verse 4a, the Hebrew is playful. It begins,

36

literally, 'A slack hand makes...' and here we might pause to consider what an idle hand could possibly 'make'. But then the phrase concludes not with 'poverty' (as we read in English translations) but with 'a pauper'. In other words, sit on your hands and you will make something—a poor man!

2 Getting real

Proverbs 11:1–19

Reading this selection of sayings through quickly, you might get the impression that many of them are pushing a fairly simplistic message, summed up by verse 5: 'The righteousness of the blameless keeps his way straight, but the wicked falls by his own wickedness.' Indeed, no less than seven of these verses (vv. 3, 5, 6, 8, 17, 18, 19) suggest that virtue is rewarded, while vice is self-defeating and ends in tears. Other verses (vv. 2, 4, 7, 9, 10) reinforce the message in slightly different ways.

We might want to believe this message, and it is undeniable that if we are diligent, sober, studious, God-fearing and trustworthy, we may prosper (all other things being equal), while the feckless, ignorant, lazy and deceitful are likely to lead miserable lives. However, whether or not it is a good thing that the devout and virtuous prosper is debatable. We may recall John Wesley's rueful words at the end of his ministry: 'In every place, the Methodists grow worldly.' Furthermore, the proposition (seemingly accepted by Proverbs) that righteousness brings prosperity is very far from being universally true. Surely poverty is the lot of many blameless people, and not all wealth is gained through truth-telling and fair dealing.

In fact, though, Proverbs is very much aware of these complications. In the midst of this stream of what might seem to be pious wishful thinking, we are brought up short by verse 16, which, in the Hebrew original, says, 'Attractive women get respect and ruthless men get wealthy.' Do not be deceived by the longer versions of this verse that are offered by many English translations (for example, NRSV). As the footnotes should tell you, the additional words come from the ancient Greek translation, whose writer could not cope with the cold splash of realism in the original and so made it say what he thought was proper.

Wisdom involves not only pressing for what the world should be, but also recognising the reality of the world we live in.

3 Your words have power

Proverbs 16:21–30

Once again, a random selection of verses from Proverbs seems to offer a jumbled miscellany of sayings. (You might want to read it through slowly and see if just one of the sayings speaks to you particularly today.) However, on closer examination of the whole passage, a hidden theme emerges, concerning the power of the human organs of speech.

The second half of verse 21, for example, links 'sweetness of lips' (a figurative expression usually understood to mean 'pleasant speech') with a wise, perceptive heart and assures us that it increases persuasiveness. Verses 23 and 24 say something very similar. Verses 27–30, on the other hand, point out that words and even some silences (the ones in which we express our disapproval eloquently enough by pursing our lips and giving a sour look) can be devastating, embittering and destroying friendships.

We might say that none of this material is very original and that it seems jumbled together with worldly-wise thoughts about the way we often pursue disastrous courses (v. 25) and are driven by our appetites (v. 26). This latter verse, however, is not as unconnected with the theme of the organs of speech as we might think. Some translations, such as the NRSV ('The appetite of workers works for them; their hunger urges them on'), obscure the connection; it is clearer in the English Standard Version, which says, 'A worker's appetite works for him; his *mouth* urges him on.' Indeed, a very literal translation might render the verse as 'A toiler's *throat* toils for him; his mouth urges him on.'

Sometimes, then, hunger and thirst compel us to act so that we can put food and drink into our mouths and satisfy involuntary cravings. On the other hand, we should be in control over what comes out of our mouths: so often, we let our tongues run away with us and come to regret our blabbing bitterly. As Jesus put it, 'What goes into someone's mouth does not defile them, but what comes out of their mouth, that is what defiles them' (Matthew 15:11, NIV).

4 Honouring wisdom where we find it

Proverbs 22:17—23:25

In 1922, the Egyptologist Adolf Erman published an article in which he claimed to have detected many similarities between an ancient Egyptian text, *The Wisdom of Amenemope*, and Proverbs 22:17—23:25. Both texts, for instance, urge their readers not to move boundary markers (a common form of fraud in ancient farming communities), to treat the poor justly, to avoid the company of hotheads, to restrain the appetite when eating with the rich and to avoid becoming rich by dishonest means. Moreover, since *Amenemope* is dated to around 1500BC, if there was a connection it seemed clear to Erman that the biblical text was reliant on the Egyptian and not the other way round.

In spite of repeated attempts to disprove Erman's theory, most scholars now believe it to be the most credible explanation of these similarities. If so, and if, like me, you have a high view of the inspiration and authority of the scriptures, we might be troubled that the Bible seems to be borrowing from a 'pagan' source.

However, the Bible itself does not seem to be so concerned about its unique authority as are some of its defenders. Paul, in Romans 1:16–23, argues that people can learn a great deal about God simply from reflecting on the created order around them (see also the similar argument in Acts 17:22–31). In fact, the biblical writers were open to the wisdom of the world around them, although they did not accept it uncritically. So if, as I believe is highly probable, Proverbs has been heavily influenced by a wise Egyptian text here, it also infuses the foreign sages' teaching with a profound devotion to the God of Israel (see, for example, 22:19, 23; 23:17), who is seen as the guarantor of all just and compassionate dealing.

If scripture itself is not so arrogant as to refuse to listen to wisdom wherever it is found, should not we be alert to 'whatever is true, whatever is honourable, whatever is just, whatever is pure, whatever is lovely, whatever is commendable' (Philippians 4:8), no matter where we find these qualities?

5 Thank God, we don't know everything

Proverbs 30:15–31

In our household we often try to control the chaos into which things tend to fall by making lists—shopping lists, 'to do' lists and Christmas card lists. When we have made a list, we can kid ourselves that we are getting things done!

The so-called 'numerical sayings' collected in this penultimate chapter of Proverbs are in a form found elsewhere in the Bible (Amos 1:3—2:8) and in texts from elsewhere in the ancient Near East. Essentially these little verses are lists, offering, so it seems, ways of organising experience and making it more manageable. They bring together similar ideas so that they can be compared and, perhaps, better understood.

It is interesting to ponder here that the Hebrew verb *mashal* (from which comes the word *meshalim*, 'proverbs', that both gives the book its title and describes its sayings) has two main meanings. It means, firstly, 'to rule' and, secondly, 'to make a comparison'. In *meshalim*, things are compared so as (we might think) to understand them better, to get a handle on them and bring them under our control.

How remarkable, then, that the first two lists before us insist that it is not so easy to count, categorise, comprehend and control reality. Verses 15b–16 offer us the grave, the barren womb (an allusion, very insensitive to our way of thinking, to the supposedly infinite yearning of a childless woman for conception), the drought-ravaged earth and an all-consuming fire as examples of things whose longing defies calculation. They point to the mystery of things seen in nature and in human relationships as beyond comprehension. These initial examples caution us against explaining the other numerical sayings too glibly—against, for instance, reading the stately walkers in verses 29–31 as simply celebrating the proud animals and the regal personage mentioned. To place a king alongside a lion in this way may be to elevate him, but what effect does it have to group the same king with a barnyard fowl and a goat? Possibly a satirical one?

In our culture we sometimes think that we can calculate everything. Thank God that mysteries remain!

6 Too good to be true?

Proverbs 31:10–31

The beginning of Proverbs is dominated by a larger-than-life semi-divine female figure, Lady Wisdom, at home in the heavenly realm; it ends with a portrait of someone who seems to be a flesh-and-blood woman, deeply involved in the life of the world. Few translations do justice to the Hebrew title *ishet hayil* that she is given in verse 10. She is far more than a 'good' or even 'excellent' or 'capable woman' (or 'wife'—the same word in Hebrew, and she is clearly married). 'Noble' or 'courageous' expresses the original more closely and, indeed, the imagery of the poem is close to the language used in paeans in praise of warriors.

The woman's struggle, however, is in the peaceful sphere of her household and community, where, through diligence and intelligent initiative, she wins prosperity for her loved ones and profound respect for herself. Proverbs has a clear view of human fallibility: again and again it warns against the pitfalls we dig for ourselves through our indolence, wickedness, vanity and stupidity. However, here, the conclusion of the book expresses a great optimism about what can happen when divine wisdom is embodied in a human life. If we fear the Lord, if we turn outward from selfish concerns and seek the good of others, we can flourish and prosper and gain the respect of the wise and good (vv. 30–31).

The poetic form used to describe this paragon, in itself, displays a sense of wholeness and completion. It is an acrostic, a device in which each line begins with the next consecutive letter in the Hebrew alphabet. So verse 10 begins with *aleph*, verse 11 with *beth*, and so on to verse 31, which begins with the 22nd and last letter, *tav*.

In this cynical age, we might be quick to suspect that verse 10 is hinting that *nowhere* can such goodness be found. Perhaps so, and only the Lord Jesus perfectly embodied virtue in a human life. Nevertheless, we must surely be open to the search for real goodness both in others and, daringly, in ourselves. Folly and vice can never gain a final victory while they are met by the goodness and wisdom of the gospel.

Guidelines

- Have we forgotten some truths, or decided to forget them, because they are inconvenient?
- 'Behind every great fortune lies a crime' (Honoré de Balzac, 1799–1850). Is this a statement of realism or cynicism? What are our responsibilities if we are fortunate enough to be wealthy?
- What have we said today that was a blessing to those who heard it? What have we said that harmed others?
- Give thanks for someone you know who is not just intelligent, but wise.
- Make a list of things that you don't understand. Which of them are mysteries that inspire wonder? Which require you to think harder.
- Reflect prayerfully on Paul's understanding that 'the foolishness of God is wiser than men' (1 Corinthians 1:25).

Mark 8:22—12:12

Earlier in the year we explored Mark 1:1—8:21. The opening chapters of Mark's Gospel introduced us to Jesus and the nature of his ministry, as well as to the disciples and Jesus' expectation of discipleship. One of the key strands of these earlier chapters is the question of response to Jesus. Three major groups (the Jewish leaders, the crowd and the disciples) all responded to Jesus stereotypically—the leaders with hostility, the crowd with amazement and the disciples with loyalty but a fundamental lack of understanding. In the midst of all this, it was the response of individuals that stood out. Where groups responded with hostility or bemusement, individuals responded genuinely, from their heart, to Jesus as he really was. Characters like the Syro-Phoenician woman and the Gerasene demoniac saw Jesus for who he was and responded to him.

This theme continues into the second half of the Gospel, where it is joined by a second, increasingly important theme. From the end of chapter 8 onwards, the Gospel moves through a gear change and the shadow of the cross looms ever larger in the story. It has been present in Mark's Gospel ever since Jesus' first conflict with the scribes in Mark 2:6–8, but it becomes more pronounced as we progress towards the end of the Gospel. Jesus' own prophecies about his death become more frequent; also more frequent are his conflicts with the Jewish authorities. These conflicts become more and more marked until Jesus' death becomes the only possible outcome.

Before we get there, however, we reach the midpoint of the Gospel, which provides a climax to some of the Gospel's key themes, the most important of all being the question of who Jesus really was.

Quotations are taken from the New Revised Standard Version of the Bible.

8–14 June

1 The healing of the blind man

Mark 8:22–26

Our first story draws our attention to one of the themes that dominate this central section of the Gospel—that of the true recognition of Jesus.

The account of the man born blind has a couple of unusual features that make it stand out from other miracles. The first is that Jesus led the man out of the village before healing him. Although, in Mark, Jesus often tells the recipient of healing not to say anything about it, the healings normally take place in public with an audience. This is one of the rare occasions when that does not happen. Another unusual feature is that the healing is not immediately successful. When Jesus asks the man what he can see, his response, 'I can see people, but they look like trees, walking' (v. 24), indicates that further healing is necessary.

Various scholars have seen both of these features as significant, given the position of this passage in Mark. Immediately before the healing, we hear a conversation between Jesus and his disciples in which Jesus exclaims, in apparent frustration, about the fact that they still do not understand the meaning of his miracles. Straight afterwards comes Peter's declaration at Caesarea Philippi that Jesus is the Messiah, followed closely by his insistence that this Messiah should not die. In both of these passages, disciples who have a close relationship with Jesus reveal that, despite the relationship, they still have a long way to go before they can see things as they really are.

Just as Jesus explains everything to the disciples in private, this man is healed in private. Just like the disciples, the man does not see things as they really are immediately: it takes some time. This observation does not make the details of the healing any less true, but it does draw our attention to the way Mark structures his narrative. As Mark unfolds his account of Jesus, he places stories very carefully within it, and the placing of these stories gives us hints about how to understand what is going on. This story, placed as it is, prepares us for the fact that the disciples may see and recognise something of who Jesus is, but it will take more than the first opening of their eyes to enable them to see the full reality.

2 You are the Messiah

Mark 8:27–33

The story of the healing of the man born blind prepares us well for what happens next. Caesarea Philippi (otherwise known as Caesarea Paneas) was in an area now known as the Golan Heights, north-east of Galilee. It was famous at the time of the Romans for its spring, which was dedicated to Pan, the Roman god of desolate places. This conversation between Jesus and his disciples was conducted, then, in a desolate place normally associated with Roman gods and not the God of Israel.

The importance of the conversation, coming as it does almost exactly in the middle of Mark's Gospel, should not be underestimated. The disciples have been with Jesus constantly; they have listened to his teaching and seen his miracles, but the question that remains is what they have made of everything that they have seen.

Jesus begins the discussion by exploring other people's thoughts about who he is. Unsurprisingly, popular opinion tries to identify him with characters who are already known. Jesus has clearly made a mark, because the people mentioned—John the Baptist and Elijah—are well-known prophets who have brought discomfiting and challenging messages. It quickly becomes clear, however, that Jesus is far more interested in the conclusions that the disciples have made for themselves.

Peter's response, 'You are the Messiah' (v. 29), is significant. Peter has recognised enough of Jesus to be able to identify him as the long-awaited Anointed One, come to save God's people. It is at this point that the significance of the story of the partially healed blind man becomes clear. Just as the blind man saw 'people... like trees, walking', Peter sees Jesus as the Messiah, but not as a Messiah who must suffer and die (v. 32). It is hardly surprising that Peter should think in this way. The long-awaited Messiah, in Jewish expectations, was often associated with a king like David who would gloriously defeat Israel's enemies and restore the fortunes of Israel to the golden days of the reign of David.

Peter has made an important connection but it does not go far enough. He sees enough to identify Jesus, correctly, as the Messiah, but not enough to realise that Jesus' Messiahship will be very different from his expectations. His vision is accurate but clouded.

3 Take up your cross

Mark 8:34–38

After Peter's outrage at the thought that the Son of Man should suffer and die, this addendum brings a crucial focus to the central part of Mark's

Gospel. Not only does Jesus think that he should suffer and die, but he also expects his followers—disciples like Peter (and us)—to take up their crosses. This section of Mark's Gospel (which runs up to 11:1 and the triumphal entry into Jerusalem) is often known by scholars as the 'way of the cross', a title that emphasises the need for his disciples, as well as Jesus, to commit themselves to sacrifice and possible death.

In the early church, this passage was perhaps misunderstood by some as a call for Christians to die for their faith, no matter what; some of the early bishops, such as Ignatius of Antioch, seem a little overkeen on martyrdom. Jesus' point here is not that we must rush towards death with enthusiasm but that the conversion (the Greek word is *metanoia*) to which Jesus calls us involves removing ourselves from the centre of our own lives and putting Jesus there instead. As verse 34 so clearly puts it, we must deny ourselves (the Greek means literally 'repudiate' or 'disown') and follow in the footsteps of Jesus. We must oust ourselves from the centre of our own lives and open ourselves in surrender to Jesus.

This surrender may or may not end in death, but that is not the point. The point is our willingness to do it. When we place ourselves at the centre of our own existence, surrendering our lives to someone else is unthinkable. It is only when we can 'disown' ourselves and, instead, be owned by Jesus that we discover what living is all about. As Jesus says here, the irony is that the more we try to save ourselves, the more likely we are to lose ourselves (v. 35). Only when we let go of our own welfare do we discover true life.

4 The transfiguration

Mark 9:1–13

In Mark's Gospel there are three moments when Jesus is revealed to be truly who he is—truly God and truly human. We noticed the first of these earlier in the year when we read the account of Jesus' baptism: as Mark recounts it, the heavens were torn apart and God spoke, saying, 'You are my Son, the Beloved; with you I am well pleased' (1:11).

Superficially, the story of the transfiguration appears different. This time, Jesus' clothes become dazzling white; the heavens are not torn apart but, instead, a cloud comes down from heaven and overshadows the people present. To the people of the first century, however, the two accounts would have sounded very similar indeed. In the Old Testament, certain phenomena were associated with God's presence, including thunder, lightning, earthquakes and clouds. So closely associated were these aspects of the weather with the presence of God that the story of Elijah on the mountain (1 Kings 19:11–12) goes out of its way to remind readers that God's presence was only associated with these phenomena: God was not actually in them.

The presence of God was also associated with garments of shining white. White clothes were considered divine because pure whiteness was very hard to achieve in the ancient world, and light was thought to shine from God's throne. Where God is described in the Old Testament, he is often associated with the colour white or with light (see, for example, Daniel 7:9).

This means that the shining white clothes and the descent of a cloud at the transfiguration send a message very similar to the tearing apart of heaven that we see in Mark 1:11. The connection between the two stories is made even stronger by the voice of God declaring Jesus to be his beloved Son.

In the space of two chapters, then, Jesus' true identity is shown. He is God, revealed as such on the top of a mountain (just as Moses encountered God on the top of a mountain, Exodus 19:20), and he is human, sent to die on a cross for those he came to save. At the heart of Mark's Gospel we hear loud and clear who Jesus is. The question that echoes to us through the centuries is Jesus' question to his disciples: 'But who do *you* say that I am?' (Mark 8:29).

5 I believe; help my unbelief

Mark 9:14–29

The episode that takes place after the transfiguration appears, to our eyes, very odd indeed. Again, in order to make sense of it, we need to reflect on the passage in the light of the other events that are described in this part of the Gospel. The healing of the blind man, Peter's declaration that Jesus is the Messiah and, most recently, the transfiguration all focus our attention on a process. The blind man began to see but needed further help to see entirely. Peter, both at Caesarea Philippi and on the mount of transfiguration, half understood but half misunderstood. He recognised Jesus to be the Messiah but refused to believe that he had to die; he saw the transfigured Jesus on the mountain and wanted to build dwelling-places so that they could all stay longer.

Here, as so often happens in Mark, the person with the greatest need of Jesus (the father of the child) sees instinctively how to respond to what is going on, and his response resonates strongly with the theme of a process: 'I believe; help my unbelief,' he exclaims (v. 24). This plea reveals that belief and unbelief are not static. The way we talk today often suggests the view that we either believe or we don't. The father's response indicates that this is not the case. Unlike Peter, who, at this stage, appears not to recognise his lack of belief, the father sees clearly that belief is dynamic and involves a measure of both believing and unbelieving at the same time.

The reason why the disciples were unable to heal the child appears opaque. If this kind of healing requires prayer (v. 29), is Jesus implying that other forms of healing do not? The answer must surely be 'no', and we need to notice that Jesus does not say whose prayer is needed for this kind of healing to be effective. After Jesus took over the healing from the disciples, the only feature that changed was that the child's father declared his faith. This suggests that the problem previously was that the father brought the child to the disciples but then passively waited for help. What changed was his own declaration of belief, even though it was limited.

6 Who is the greatest?

Mark 9:30–37

If we are left in any doubt that the disciples are struggling to believe as they should, the next story points directly to this theme. Despite the amount of time they have spent with Jesus, they start to argue among themselves about who is the most important. Clearly their recognition of the demands of discipleship still leaves a lot to be desired. However, verse 34 indicates that they are, at least, aware of how embarrassing their position is, since they fall into silence when Jesus asks them what they are talking about.

This situation offers Jesus the cue to talk about one of the most crucial aspects of discipleship—a willingness to be the servant of other people. As Jesus places a child in their midst in this context, he is focusing their attention entirely on the question of social importance. In Jesus' society, a child was seen as of very little importance. Indeed, the Greek words for 'children' were of neuter gender: people were not regarded as fully gendered human beings until they reached puberty. Jesus' action, therefore, is a reminder that to be his follower demands countercultural and counter-intuitive behaviour.

Now, as then, our natural course of behaviour is to treat best those who will be able to respond in kind. Jesus' point is that a child cannot respond to be of any use to us. Children have no property and no influence and, in his day, were seen as having value only in the future.

True discipleship, then, involves forgetting one's own needs and desires and focusing instead on the needs and desires of those who are least able to reciprocate. The people who do that are those who will be first in God's kingdom.

Guidelines

The themes that we have explored this week provide a bracing challenge to those of us who are seeking to live faithfully as Christians. In them we are called to remove ourselves from the centre of our own lives and to place Christ there instead. We are called to seek out those in our society who are least valued and least able to reciprocate, and then to serve them. We are also called to recognise that the road to true discipleship is long and winding. Even Jesus' own disciples took a long time to recognise who he really was, rather than who they wanted him to be.

The cry of the epileptic child's father is one that we should all take deeply to heart. No matter how long we have been Christians and no matter how certain we feel about our faith, there will be corners of our lives where we need greater responsiveness, deeper love and more faith. Just like the disciples, who, time and time again, demonstrated that they didn't fully comprehend who Jesus was, each one of us needs to journey further into faith and trust in God and to echo the father's words: 'Lord, I believe; help my unbelief.'

1 Whoever is not against us is for us

Mark 9:38–50

It is a natural part of human nature to enquire whether someone is 'one of us' or not. Our instinct tells us to trust them if the answer is 'yes' and to spurn them if the answer is 'no'. The apparently miscellaneous sayings of Jesus in Mark 9:38–48 all address this instinct. What really matters in the kingdom of God is not whom or what you belong to, but the effects of what you do in the world in which you live.

The first example involves someone who is casting out demons in the name of Jesus but not following him. Jesus' instruction not to stop the exorcist is somewhat surprising. Surely only those who follow Jesus should use his power? Jesus' answer reminds us that it is the power, not the person using it, that is important. If it really is Jesus' power that they are using, they will not be able to speak against him (v. 39), and if they can't speak against him, they are for him (v. 40). In other words, the proof is in the person's actions, not his proclaimed allegiances.

Conversely, there is nothing that belongs to you quite so much as your hand, foot or eye (vv. 43–47). But if any part of you acts against Jesus rather than for him, then the whole to which it belongs will be deemed to be against him. If that part is against him, ultimately the whole will suffer the fate of those who are against him. For this reason it is wise to remove from ourselves whatever might hint at opposition to Jesus. Again, what is important is not so much whom you say you belong to, but what you reveal about yourself by what you do.

Verses 49–50 are very hard to understand in their context, as they don't obviously fit with the other sayings, beyond the superficial connection with fire. Verses 43 and 47 speak of being cast into the fire of Gehenna (or 'hell') and in verse 49 it is stated that everyone will be salted with fire. Elsewhere in the Bible, fire is used as a picture of trials that must be suffered (1 Peter 1:6–7), and salt is a preservative. As a result, this odd little couplet may mean that salt (that is, faith) is needed to preserve you against the trials you will face, but what will happen if you have lost your faith, the source of that preservation?

2 Divorce and adultery

Mark 10:1–12

Over the years, Jesus' teaching on divorce has produced a vast amount of controversy and heartache as Christians have attempted to work out what they should understand from it in today's society. Each Christian needs to come to his or her own position on what it means for us today, but a few historical comments may help to place it in clearer perspective.

Divorce was as controversial in the first century as it is today, but one of the key things to bear in mind is how different that culture was from our own. In the world of the Old and New Testaments, laws about marriage and divorce were primarily concerned to protect those who were most vulnerable in society. A woman was the property of her father until she became the property of her husband. If, for some reason, her husband did not like her and turned her out for unimportant reasons, she would become destitute, with no one to turn to for shelter. A bill of divorce provided some level of protection. It meant that the husband could not divorce her for any trivial reason and had to establish, before witnesses, a proper reason for his desire to divorce her.

By the time of Jesus, a rabbinic discussion about divorce had developed, with differing views about what counted as a 'valid reason' for divorce. Two rabbis in particular were well known for their contrasting opinions. Rabbi Shammai argued that a woman could be divorced only for the most serious of transgressions, whereas Rabbi Hillel allowed divorce for something as trivial as burning a meal.

Jesus' view, stated here, offers the most protection to women. There is no offence serious enough to allow a man to withdraw food, shelter and support from a woman (although it is worth noting that Matthew 5:32 adds a rider, allowing 'unchastity' as the sole reason for divorce).

Jesus' protection of the weakest and most vulnerable members of society is characteristic of him. The question for us today is who within our society are the weakest and most vulnerable, and how do we ensure that their rights and needs are cared for?

3 Let the children come to me

Mark 10:13–16

It is easy to confuse this passage about children with the passage we read last week from Mark 9:30–37. They are both, after all, about children—but the point in Mark 10 is quite different. The focus of Mark 9:30–37 is greatness (or lack of it). There, Jesus was explaining that the calling of discipleship is to be a servant to others, especially to those, like children, who cannot reciprocate. Here in Mark 10, he is making another point. This passage is not about whom you serve but about how you receive the kingdom.

The social context is, of course, the same: the disciples' outrage about the bringing of children to Jesus for blessing may well be connected with children's low status within their society. The disciples don't want Jesus to be troubled by such an insignificant task, but Jesus responds with characteristic insight. The grammar of the sentence in verse 15 is slightly unclear, but Jesus seems to be saying that whoever does not receive the kingdom in the way that a child receives the kingdom will not enter it. In other words, we can enter the kingdom only if we adopt a child-like attitude.

Jesus' command requires us to think imaginatively about what it might be like to receive the kingdom as a child would receive it. What characteristics does this require of us? Trust? Innocence? Joy? Lack of status? The list could go on but, first and foremost, it requires us to place great value on what others perceive to be of little value.

Jesus goes on to demonstrate this attitude. The parents of the children have brought them for a blessing. What they have in mind is probably something quite formal and distant, requiring Jesus simply to stretch out his hand to bless them. Instead, he catches them up in a hug. The word translated as 'took them up in his arms' (v. 16) also means 'hugged' or 'embraced'. This is an act of great tenderness and compassion. As is so often the case, Jesus far exceeds the expectations of the people he meets. These parents expect a simple blessing but, instead, experience profound tenderness and care.

4 Give away everything you own

Mark 10:17–22

The theme exploring the characteristics of true discipleship continues in this passage with an even more uncomfortable message. The character described by Mark simply as 'a man' (v. 17), who turns out, at the end of the account, to be very rich, is popularly known as the 'rich young ruler'. He is described as rich in all three accounts of his meeting with Jesus (the other two being Matthew 19:16–22 and Luke 18:18–24). The epithet 'young' comes from Matthew 19:20 and 'ruler' is found in Luke 18:18.

The man's question is an interesting one: what must he do to inherit eternal life? A similar question is asked of Jesus in Luke 10:25–28, where Jesus corrects the wording in his response: 'do this, and you will live'. The lawyer who asks the question in this case sees eternal life as an external commodity that can be earned in the same way that bread or a reputation can be earned. If he does the right thing, he believes, he will be able to receive it. As Jesus points out, however, if he truly follows the command to love God and his neighbour (Luke 10:27), he will begin to live right away.

In Mark 10, too, Jesus changes the focus of the man's emphasis. The rich man believes that eternal life can be earned by proper obedience to the law. Jesus does not disagree but, instead, focuses his response on discovering how much this man really wants what he claims to want. What is he prepared to give up in order to receive eternal life? It turns out that his money means more to him than eternal life, so he goes away saddened. It is an intriguing exchange. Jesus' response, Mark tells us, arises out of love, not condemnation (v. 21), and suggests that the man lacks something important.

As we discover, on one level, this rich man lacks for nothing, but his question to Jesus in the first place indicates that he himself feels a lack in his life. If he did not, why would he enquire about eternal life? Jesus, seeing his lack, knows exactly what he needs, but his response is far from what the man wants to hear. He wants to be told that he can keep all his possessions *and* receive eternal life: keeping what he has is more important to him than gaining what he lacks.

5 Entering the kingdom of God

Mark 10:23–31

Jesus continues the theme of the story of the rich man, and explains to the disciples what it means: people with wealth will find it very difficult to enter the kingdom of heaven. The disciples' astonishment at this claim suggests that they, like many Jews of their time, saw wealth as a sign of God's blessing. Indeed, they may have believed that wealth enabled them to worship God properly. If they were wealthy, they could avoid impurity more easily and would also have more liberty to cleanse themselves afterwards. In short, the wealthier they were, the holier they could be.

If this is how the disciples perceived the issue, it would have been very difficult for them to imagine a context in which wealth made access to God difficult, if not impossible (v. 25). Much has been made in commentaries of the claim that there was a small gate in Jerusalem called the Needle Gate, suggesting that Jesus may have been referring to this gate rather than an actual needle. Few New Testament scholars today would support such an interpretation, not least because there is no evidence for the existence of the gate. (The idea originated from a footnote in a commentary written in the ninth century.) It is much more likely that Jesus intended his illustration to describe something completely impossible: there is a similar saying in rabbinic literature, about an elephant going through the eye of a needle.

As the ongoing conversation between Jesus and Peter makes clear, by leaving behind riches, we are enabled to enter the kingdom. Once we have entered, we receive the untold wealth of different family relationships, hospitality and generosity. We leave behind one father and mother and gain many, many more in the kingdom. The willingness to leave everything behind means that we have the capacity to enjoy true treasure—the treasure of the family of God (v. 30; although, as Mark mentions, even this comes 'with persecutions' until God's dominion is established).

The final verse brings us to the topsy-turvy values of the kingdom, in which the first is last and the last first. In the kingdom, there are untold riches for those who want them, but these are the kingdom's riches—the pearls of justice, the gems of peace and the gold bars of love. It is essential to cast off a love of money before entering, because, unless we do, we will be unable to appreciate the true treasure chest of the kingdom.

6 Sitting on the right and left of God

Mark 10:32–45

As the disciples accompany Jesus towards Jerusalem, the shadow of his cross falls ever more deeply across their journey. Once more, Jesus prophesies his death and resurrection, and again the disciples misunderstand his meaning. To our eye, the question of James and John appears to be an entire non sequitur. How could they get from the threat of mockery and death to ideas about sitting on either side of Jesus in his glory? The reality appears to be that Jesus was talking about his death but they heard him talking about coming into his glorious kingdom. As we now know, they were right: at his death and resurrection, Jesus did come into his Father's kingdom. However, just like the riches of the kingdom that we considered in the previous passage, the glory of Jesus' kingdom is to be found in self-sacrificial suffering and death.

The whole of Jesus' conversation with James and John is laden with irony. Jesus knows, Mark knows and we know the implications of the two disciples' request. The only ones who, apparently, do not know are James and John themselves. Their request, to sit one on the right- and one on the left-hand side of the king, means being granted the highest honour in the kingdom—to be regarded as vice-regents who will rule alongside the king. What they don't know is that the moment when Jesus will come into his kingship will be at his crucifixion (where he was indeed described as the King of the Jews). There, the spaces to his right and his left will be occupied by two bandits (see Mark 15:26–27).

The upside is that, in the topsy-turvy kingdom of God, there is plenty of space for people to sit at the right and left hand of Jesus, and, when they do, they will indeed share in his glory. The downside is that this glory is experienced through self-giving and the willingness to lay down one's life for others.

Guidelines

This week's passages from Mark have all highlighted the theme of the true character of Christian discipleship. The theme that has been growing slowly throughout the Gospel now comes to the fore. Right at the start of Mark, the disciples took their first step into discipleship—they followed

Jesus—but, as the story has progressed, it has become increasingly clear that this was only a first step. In chapters 4—8 it became clear that Jesus had other expectations of the disciples as well: he expected them to understand both who he was and the message that he had come to bring.

In chapters 9—10, the cost of discipleship has become the focus. It is not enough just to follow Jesus. It is not even enough to comprehend his message. Those who follow Jesus must be prepared to lay down their lives, as he is prepared to do. They must be prepared to give up all they hold dear for the sake of the kingdom. They must be prepared to give up status and prestige and become like children.

Jesus' message is as uncomfortable today as it was to the disciples then, and his challenge still rings in our ears: how much are we prepared to give up in order to enter the kingdom of God? Given the topsy-turvy values of the kingdom, are we prepared to let go of our 'rights' in order to receive the riches that God has in store for us or, like the rich man, will the cost prove too great for us?

1 My teacher

Mark 10:46–52

Today's passage contains the final healing narrative in Mark's Gospel, which is also the final episode in Jesus' ministry before the story of his passion begins. It is interesting, therefore, that this is another story about sight (see 8:22–26). Here again, Mark places a story in his Gospel not only because it is important in itself but also because it allows him to draw attention to themes that make sense of the rest of the narrative. We are reminded here that a physical lack of sight is not the only type of blindness. The disciples and the Jewish leaders are inwardly blind and need healing just as much as Bartimaeus does, but they have not noticed.

Bartimaeus' persistence stands out, along with his certainty that Jesus can help him. Although his cry to Jesus is quoted only twice by Mark (vv. 47–48), the text implies that he both started and continued to shout out, and, having annoyed the people around him, carried on doing it some more.

His request to Jesus is also interesting. There are only two places in the

New Testament where Jesus is addressed as 'Rabbouni' or 'My teacher' (v. 51). The other is in John 20:16, where Mary sees the resurrected Jesus. The simpler word 'Rabbi' is used much more commonly (about 15 times), but 'Rabbouni' is a heightened form, implying a strong relationship. This means that Bartimaeus shouldn't really have called Jesus 'Rabbouni'. We can see why Mary might have called him 'my teacher' but the details in Bartimaeus' story suggest that he had not met Jesus before. However, it would appear that Bartimaeus not only recognised what Jesus could do for him ('let me see again') but also knew that this entailed a personal relationship with Jesus. So clear was this realisation that he used the more personal form of address before Jesus had done anything at all.

The stories that follow this one in Mark take us towards Jesus' death and resurrection. Here, in the story of Bartimaeus, we meet an individual who not only knows his need of Jesus but also recognises that with the meeting of that need comes a deep relationship.

2 Riding on a donkey

Mark 11:1–6

As we have travelled through Mark, the cross has cast an ever deeper shadow across Jesus' life and ministry. We have already noticed how his prophecies about his own death have increased in the course of the Gospel. Now we reach the point of no return. Jesus has come to Jerusalem and his death is imminent.

In Matthew, Mark and Luke, this is Jesus' first recorded visit to Jerusalem as an adult (Luke 2 includes the story of his childhood visit to the temple). John's Gospel is the only one to suggest that Jesus has visited Jerusalem regularly, during the major festivals. Indeed, it is from John's Gospel that the tradition of a three-year ministry arises. John reports that Jesus made three separate visits to Jerusalem for the annual Passover celebration. Matthew, Mark and Luke simply have two main locations for Jesus' life and ministry—Galilee and Jerusalem (with a journey between the two also indicated). It is highly unlikely, however, that Jesus only visited Jerusalem once: he would have been expected to attend the three major festivals of the year, so John's Gospel is probably the most accurate in this case.

A familiarity with Jerusalem is indicated by the fact that Jesus has made prior arrangements for the use of a donkey on his entry into the city (vv. 2–3). The wording implies that Jesus knows the owners of the donkey and has arranged in advance for them to loan him the animal. Who they were and what connection they had with Jesus are unknown, other than that, like Mary, Martha and Lazarus, they lived in Bethany. It is not impossible that the donkey's owners were, in fact, Mary, Martha and Lazarus, but we cannot know for sure.

The donkey is, of course, highly significant to our understanding of what is going on here. A victorious Roman general would ride on a white horse as a symbol of his victory. Jewish tradition, however, looked forward to the king coming not only in victory but also in humility (Zechariah 9:9). In acknowledgement that the victory belonged to God and not himself, their king would ride not a fine white horse but a humble donkey. Jesus' riding on a donkey, then, was momentous. In riding the donkey, he indicated to the crowds not only that he was the long-awaited king but also that any victory they might perceive in him should be attributed to God.

3 Hosanna!

Mark 11:7–11

The words sung by the crowd around Jesus as he moves towards Jerusalem (vv. 9–10) are also important. They are taken from Psalm 118:25–26. One feature to notice is the phrase translated 'Save us' in the psalm. This is the English translation of the Hebrew *Hoshiah na* (literally, 'save now'), which, when transliterated into Greek, reads *Hosanna*. The song of the crowd, therefore, is a Greek version of the psalm. Psalm 118 comes from a collection known as the Hallel Psalms (Psalms 113—118), which were traditionally sung during the pilgrimage to Jerusalem and also during the Passover meal. This means that the crowd may have been singing Psalm 118 anyway, during their pilgrimage to Jerusalem, and, in singing it, may suddenly have realised what was going on before their very eyes as Jesus rode his donkey towards the city.

The other important feature of Psalm 118 is that it recorded a king's victory from the past. No one is sure who this king was, but verses 1–18 recount the dangerous battle that the king faced until God saved him. The second half of the psalm (vv. 19–29) describes the king's triumphant return to Jerusalem to worship God in the temple, giving thanks for all that God has done for him.

Historically, verses 25 and 26 would have been spoken by two different groups of people. Verse 25, 'Save us, we beseech you, O Lord! O Lord, we beseech you, give us success', may well have been said by the crowd that accompanied the king on his return, praying that God would save them too and grant them success. Then, verse 26, 'Blessed is the one who comes in the name of the Lord. We bless you from the house of the Lord', would have been the response of the priests in the temple. They recognised the coming of the king and blessed him from the temple itself.

In the context of Mark's Gospel, this becomes very important. After entering Jerusalem, Jesus goes straight to the temple—where nothing happens. Jesus simply looks around and leaves (v. 11). His experience stands in stark contrast to Psalm 118, where the priests recognise the king for who he is and bless him. The theme of the failure of the priests and the temple officials to acknowledge Jesus becomes an important one as Mark's story unfolds.

4 The fig tree and the temple

Mark 11:12–25

The account of Jesus' cursing of the fig tree in verses 12–20 may well be one of the oddest stories in the whole Gospel. On the surface, there seems to be little point to it other than to display a most unreasonable fit of pique from Jesus, who, annoyed by a tree that was not fruiting (out of season), curses it so that it dies. The story begins to make sense only when we realise that Mark tells it in order to help us understand all the other events going on around.

Fig trees were often used in the Old Testament to symbolise the future blessing that Israel would receive from God (see, for example, Zechariah 3:10). The fig tree in fruit symbolised a lavish blessing, while a fig tree lacking fruit or with withered fruit, conversely, symbolised a curse (see Jeremiah 8:13; 29:17). It is also worth knowing that fig trees have on them both this year's fruit and the buds of next year's fruit at the same time. In other words, finding no fruit or buds at all on the tree meant that there was no chance it would bear fruit in the foreseeable future.

In Mark's Gospel, the story of the cursing of the fig tree is carefully wrapped around the narrative of the cleansing of the temple. On the evening of the triumphal entry, Jesus goes into the temple, looks around and leaves. First thing the next morning, he curses the fig tree. He then goes back into the temple and overturns the tables of the money changers. Next day, he discovers that the fig tree has now withered. The fig tree is cursed for not doing what it should be doing—producing fruit. By extension, Mark appears to be nudging us to understand that the temple is also not doing what it should do. The temple is meant to be a house of prayer for all the nations but instead has been made into a den of robbers (v. 17).

Just as Jesus saw that the fig tree would never produce the fruit it should produce, so he saw that the temple would not produce fruit either. It had lost its way, so Jesus condemned it, just as he had condemned the fig tree.

5 A question of authority

Mark 11:25–33

The question about Jesus' authority has rumbled on through the Gospel ever since Mark 1:22, when Jesus first taught in the synagogue in Capernaum, and 2:1–12, where he was challenged over his authority to forgive sins. The issue there was that he spoke as though he had authority, but it was not an authority that anyone at the time recognised. The question now comes to a head in Mark 11. The chief priests, the scribes and the elders want to know where Jesus thinks his authority comes from.

On one level, this is a legitimate question. The chief priests, scribes and elders all held their positions because authority had been given to them by human structures. The temple officials and the Jewish leadership used various methods to identify those to whom authority would be given: sometimes it was on the basis of a family line and sometimes on the basis of experience. The problem is that Jesus stands outside all these human structures and lines of authority, so his position is not recognised. The question, then, is fair enough: what makes him think he has the authority to speak and act as he does?

Jesus appears to have the annoying tendency to avoid answering the questions put to him. More often than not, he answers a question with another question. He does exactly that here in verse 30, but it is worth noticing that his question does provide us with an answer, even if it did nothing for the original inquisitors.

Jesus clearly knows that John was perceived by the people to have had authority from heaven, but the authorities have no intention of acknowledging this fact. The same is true of Jesus, and his questioning 'answer' draws the truth of the issue into the forefront. If the authority of both John and Jesus truly comes from heaven—as the people believe—then the human authorities ought to acknowledge it and ascribe him human authority too. The chief priests, scribes and elders are not saying what they mean. What they really want to say is that Jesus has no authority of any kind but they are too cowardly to voice that opinion. Jesus, with his usual skill, reveals the duplicity of their question and rightly refuses to collude in it.

6 The parable of the tenants

Mark 12:1–12

Ever since the entry into Jerusalem, the conflict between Jesus and the Jewish authorities has been getting worse. Our final passage in this section of our exploration of Mark's Gospel sees the conflict reach uncontrollable proportions. Where, before, Jesus' criticism of the Jewish authorities has been oblique and indirect, here it is explicit. Even more importantly, the chief priests, scribes and elders recognise the serious nature of Jesus' criticism of them and decide to arrest him.

The parable of the tenants reveals to the people of Jesus' day, as well as to us, what has gone wrong in the leadership of God's people. In short, as the parable so ably demonstrates, the leaders (identified as the tenants in the parable) have forgotten that their charge is held on behalf of God and not in their own right. Their attitude links back to the question about authority in the previous passage. The question by the Jewish leaders implied that, since they themselves had not given Jesus authority, he could have no authority. What they had forgotten was that they held their authority on trust from God. Similarly, their care of the vineyard should be exercised on his behalf and not for their own benefit.

The parable of the tenants helps us to understand Jesus' comment in Mark 11:17 that God's house should be a house of prayer for all the nations but that 'you have made it a den of robbers'. The Greek word used for 'robbers' here is the word not just for thieves but for political bandits. There were people in Jesus' day who were 'bandits': their sole purpose was to overthrow the Romans and rule the people themselves. The parable of the tenants seems to make clear that this is Jesus' criticism of the Jewish leaders. They should be caring for all the nations and guiding them to God. Instead they have, effectively, staged a coup and care only about their own position and status. They have become bandits, seeking to overthrow God and rule in his stead. It is hardly surprising, then, that the Jewish leaders decide to kill Jesus after they have understood the extent of his criticism of them.

Guidelines

Chapters 10—12 move us one step closer to Jesus' final conflict with the Jewish authorities, the conflict that will ultimately lead to his death. As we move towards Jesus' death, the nature of this conflict becomes clearer and clearer. Jesus came proclaiming that God's kingdom was breaking into the world. This was a kingdom marked by the principles of God—justice, peace and righteousness. At all times in history, there are those who welcome that kingdom with joy, those who flee from it in fear and those who resist it with every fibre of their being. By and large, those who welcome it with joy either have little to lose or so clearly recognise the glory of what is on offer that they happily let go of what they have.

In great contrast, those with much to lose in terms of power or wealth resist God's kingdom. The Jewish leaders of Jesus' day fell into this category. Whatever their views of Jesus, they simply had too much to lose to allow themselves to recognise him and the kingdom he proclaimed. It is easy to condemn them for this blinkered attitude, but, if we do so, we may be in danger of falling into the same trap. It would be far wiser to reflect long and hard on the ways in which we might be acting as they did. Those of us with much to lose often resist God's kingdom even now, without realising that we do so.

FURTHER READING

Elizabeth Malbon, *Hearing Mark: A listener's guide*, Continuum, 2002.

Ben Witherington III, *The Gospel of Mark: Socio-rhetorical commentary*, Eerdmans, 2001.

Tom Wright, *Mark for Everyone*, SPCK, 2001.

Esther and post-Christendom

Although we often hear it said today that we live in a 'post-Christian world', the phrase is somewhat misleading. In a truly 'post-Christian' world, the Christian faith itself will have ceased to exist. Yet Christian faith is alive and well and, in most of the world, it is clearly growing.

On the other hand, many people do now openly reject not only the Christian faith but all faith. On some Christmas billboards in 2012, American atheists showed pictures of Santa and Jesus with the text 'Keep the Merry! Dump the Myth!' Their suggestion was that Jesus, not Santa Claus, is the myth we should drop. Meanwhile, in Britain, atheists campaign for atheism to be included in the Religious Education syllabus in schools.

Alongside this rejection of faith, whereas 'religion' was once more or less equivalent to 'Christianity' in the West, it is now the case that 'religion' refers to many faiths, and Christianity is no longer in a privileged position. The kind of society in which Christianity holds a privileged position—known as Christendom—is now past. What distinguishes post-Christendom from the past is that people of all faiths and no faith may now speak from equal, unprivileged positions.

In this context, the book of Esther is particularly important. Although best known as the only book of the Bible that does not directly mention God, it should perhaps be better known as the only book of the Old Testament that mentions neither the temple nor the land of Israel. It focuses instead on the Jews who remained in Babylon after King Cyrus had granted them permission to return to their homeland. Their faith had been privileged in the land of Israel, but here it was just one among many. These exiles lived in a society where, instead of understanding Yahweh alone as being God, other people regarded their own gods as being equally (or even more) valid. So Esther explores a world that, although distant from ours in many ways, is also similar to the Western world today. In doing so, it models one way in which faith might be worked out in the face of extraordinary opposition—by people living counterculturally and subtly pointing to the wider story of scripture.

Quotations are taken from the New Revised Standard Version of the Bible unless otherwise indicated.

1 Speaking truth about power

Esther 1

Ahasuerus (called Xerxes in some translations) was a powerful king, and one thing the powerful like to do is to display their power. For Ahasuerus, his display took the form of an extended celebration, over a period of six months, to show the 'pomp of his majesty' (v. 4). When it ended, a further seven days were taken for an additional party at the palace to show off his wealth.

These were not simple celebrations; they were declarations to both the general population and the ruling elite that their king was someone of immense wealth and power, a man not to be challenged, whose advisers existed mainly to tell him what he wanted to hear. We see something similar today in the military parades of North Korea or, closer to home, product launches by corporate behemoths whose profits are not to be challenged by wider ethical issues.

However, just at the point when Ahasuerus seems irresistible, his wife, Vashti, refuses to join him at his celebrations. We are not told her reasons but, because the king's command was issued publicly (through the seven eunuchs, v. 10), her refusal demonstrates publicly that he is not all-powerful after all. In addition, by stating that Ahasuerus summoned Vashti while he was 'merry with wine' (v. 10), the author of Esther alludes to two previous incidents (1 Samuel 25:36; 2 Samuel 13:28) in which drunkenness preceded a powerful man's downfall. The king's advisers may fawn over him, but his wife's behaviour shows that his claims do not stand up, and the echoes of previous history give warning of his limits.

Those who challenge power directly often find themselves silenced and excluded (as, indeed, did Queen Vashti, v. 19). So the book of Esther opts for a less direct way of exposing the king's folly, partly by using satire to mock him in subtle ways. This is evident from the fact that he always accepts the advice he is given, no matter how foolish it is. This approach shows the flaws in the dominant power structure while inviting people to explore a different story. Christian witness to post-Christendom may need to do the same.

2 Countercultural faith

Esther 2:1–18

Esther herself is not mentioned in chapter 1, although Vashti's deposition allows for her rise. She does not rise because of any ambition on her part. Instead, she is caught up in the conspicuous consumption of the Persian empire, where the king's search for a new queen involves bringing many beautiful virgins into the palace for twelve months of beauty treatments, in preparation for one night with the king. Although this episode is routinely presented as a beauty contest, we can reasonably conclude that neither appearance nor conversation was what the king assessed in his night with each girl. We see here an extraordinary level of expenditure to keep one man satisfied—an expenditure that ruined the lives of many beautiful young girls and simultaneously prevented many young men from marrying, as the girls would be kept in the harem thereafter as a royal 'possession'.

It is against this background that we meet Mordecai and Esther. Mordecai is descended from someone exiled by the Babylonians, whose family has chosen to remain in exile. He has not abandoned his Jewish faith, however, and has adopted his orphaned cousin, Esther. The Bible points to God's concern for the orphan (for example, Exodus 22:22; Deuteronomy 10:18), and Mordecai lives out this concern by caring for Esther. Likewise, Esther lives out the command to honour one's parents (Exodus 20:12) in her obedience to her adoptive father, Mordecai, as she keeps secret her Jewish identity (v. 20). The behaviour of Esther and Mordecai points to a way of life that was different from the norm. It would have involved hard choices, as Esther would not have been able to have a kosher lifestyle, but it was countercultural in the fundamentals, refusing the abusive consumption that typified the palace (v. 15). In the midst of these surroundings, Esther found favour with her guardian (v. 9) and ultimately with the king (v. 17).

There is nothing to suggest that Esther would have chosen her situation, and it is clear that faith does not keep God's people from hardship, but this passage suggests that there is a life of faith that is radically countercultural. This life of faithfulness to God may ultimately find favour while challenging the dominant culture in which we find ourselves.

3 Pain from the past

Events from the distant past often shape events today. I remember an Albanian student from Kosovo explaining how the conflict with Serbia reaches back into medieval times. The events of that dreadful war emerged from hatred that reached back across the centuries, and memories of past hurts led to appalling levels of new violence.

Such memories are important here in Esther 3. When Mordecai was introduced (2:5) we were given his genealogy, presented in a way that echoes King Saul's (1 Samuel 9:1). We might expect him to be rewarded for saving the king's life (2:19–23), but instead we see the sudden promotion of Haman—and Haman is an 'Agagite' (3:1). In other words, he is descended from the Amalekite king whom Saul failed to destroy, a failure that led to Saul's rejection as king of Israel (1 Samuel 15). The Amalekites were the first people to attack Israel after Israel had left Egypt, and had been considered God's enemies ever since (Exodus 17:8–16).

Memories of an old conflict were stirred by Mordecai's refusal to bow to Haman (v. 2), and the trouble escalated when Haman, discovering that Mordecai was Jewish, decided to destroy all the empire's Jews (v. 6). Haman cast lots to find the lucky day for this destruction, but readers know from Proverbs 16:33 that it is really Yahweh who determines the outcome of the lot. Haman tried to manipulate events—and certainly manipulated the king—to issue an edict for the destruction of all the Jews, but he could not manipulate God. Although the year between the issuing of the decree and the date when it was to be carried out would have undoubtedly been a period of great fear, it also allowed time for a change of plan.

We do not yet see a resolution of the conflict, and the decree remains harsh, but chapter 3 hints that God's purposes are greater than Haman recognises. Living as a people without power means holding on to this tension, in which we experience much that seems contrary to faith and yet, by reading events through the framework of scripture, we can see pointers to a God who can still be trusted.

4 Risking all for faith

Haman's edict to destroy all Jews had been issued, but, because Esther had obeyed Mordecai and not revealed her ethnicity, he did not know that there was a Jew in the palace. Queens did not exercise direct power but could often influence events. Would Esther oppose Haman's plans or take the safe path of continuing to hide her ethnicity?

Because life in the palace was largely isolated from the rest of the city, Esther might not have known about Haman's edict. She might have been unable to read, so, even if she saw a copy, she might not have understood its contents. But the palace was not as closed off as it might have seemed, and Mordecai could contact her through the eunuchs working there, challenging her to act for her people. Her location in the palace did not mean that Esther had easy access to the king. Indeed, his ardour for her seems to have cooled (v. 11). In Mordecai's mind, however, Esther had to be in the palace for a reason that pointed beyond herself, even if he would not say explicitly that God had put her there (v. 14).

In spite of the risk to her own life, Esther eventually took up Mordecai's challenge, calling for a fast from her people as she prepared to go to the king. The book's chronology suggests that this fast occurred at Passover. At this time, Israelites normally celebrated God's great act of deliverance, but now they fasted, as they needed another.

Esther was about to risk all for her faith, but it was a faith grounded in a God who had delivered his people in the past. It was also a risk for which she had prepared herself through a serious fast, because she knew the story of the God who delivers. Our own situation, as people who know the God who raised his Son Jesus from the dead and who sends his Spirit, reminds us that we too can challenge our circumstances. Like Esther, we do so from a position of weakness, yet we serve a God who has delivered and will deliver his people.

5 God's coincidences

Esther 6:1–13

William Temple famously observed, 'When I pray, coincidences happen; when I don't, they don't.' Of course, because the book of Esther resists any direct reference to God, it also refrains from mentioning prayer, but Esther's fast (4:16) is intended to highlight the exiles' plight before God. An appeal to God was certainly needed, because, although Esther seems to have had the king at the point of agreeing to her requests in chapter 5, later that night Haman hatched a plan to execute Mordecai by impaling him on a massive stake (v. 4: most commentators agree that this is a more likely method of execution than 'hanging' as we understand it). Mordecai's death would have made all other successes hollow for Esther, while also showing that, despite all her careful planning, she could not guarantee the desired outcome. Indeed, Esther herself is unaware that all these things are happening.

And yet, on that very night, 'sleep escaped the king' (6:1, HCSB). On that night he discovered that, some time previously, Mordecai had saved his life and had never been rewarded. While this was happening, Haman was erecting the stake on which to impale Mordecai, and he arrived at court early to ask the king's permission for the execution. So, just when the king needed his advice, Haman was present and was called in. However, his own ego prevented him from realising that the one the king wanted to honour was the one he, Haman, was preparing to execute. Even worse, he had to honour Mordecai publicly in the city before going home to hear his wife assure him that if Mordecai was Jewish, then Mordecai was bound to triumph over him.

The key factor throughout this chapter is timing. Everything happens exactly when it is required, yet God's people remain unaware of how everything is changing behind the scenes. These 'coincidences' point to a God who acts for his people in ways beyond what they might think or ask. Furthermore, Haman's wife, Zeresh, could see something about the Jews that pointed to a power with them that was greater than even the most powerful men in the empire. Even when we are not conscious of it, God is actively working on behalf of his people, and others can see it happening.

6 Putting things right

Finishing a job is often surprisingly difficult, especially if it has reached the point where we can live with a few rough edges. Esther could have been satisfied with saving herself and Mordecai, but that would not have been enough. Haman, whose pride contributed to his downfall, was defeated personally (7:10), but this did not mean the end of the evil he had set in motion. Esther and Mordecai needed to complete their work together. For Esther, this meant introducing the king to Mordecai, with all the required tact, leading to Mordecai's appointment as Haman's replacement (8:2). For Mordecai, it meant resolving the problem of the irrevocable Persian law in order to reverse Haman's decree.

Mordecai's solution is notable for its simplicity and creativity, using all the resources of the empire, just as Haman had done, to issue a counter-edict. He could not revoke the initial decree, but he could offer an alternative that effectively nullified it. His counter-edict echoed Haman's own wording, offering the Jews the chance to gather and defend themselves. Where Haman's edict was aggressive, Mordecai's was defensive. The Jews were not permitted to attack, only to defend themselves against aggressors (although chapter 9 might suggest that, in practice, not everyone observed this limit).

There was a remarkable response to Mordecai's intervention, as people celebrated with joy and feasting. Even more remarkable, many 'declared themselves Jews' (v. 17, ESV). Perhaps these declarations stemmed from the sort of fear expressed by Haman's wife, Zeresh (v. 17; 6:13), and they may not have represented a permanent change. However, we can see that, as God's people demonstrated a different lifestyle, it profoundly affected the rest of the empire.

It is perhaps surprising that a book that never mentions God should describe a response like this, but Esther suggests that a life lived in faithfulness to God, a life that points to the larger story of what God is doing, might change the people around us. These people may not have come to a full understanding but they recognise the distinctiveness of God's people. Perhaps, as God's people today continue to model such a life, we too might have an impact on our society in ways we don't expect.

Guidelines

Although Esther tackles some extremely serious issues, it frequently does so with great humour, and by referencing other parts of the Old Testament, including the Joseph story (in which Joseph, like Mordecai, acts as an adviser to a foreign king) and the exodus (Esther's fast takes place during Passover). It also echoes the book of Proverbs: Haman often seems to represent the fool (see Proverbs 12:16; 14:8; 15:14; 20:3; 26:8; 27:3; 29:9, 11), while Esther and Mordecai live out what it means to be wise (Proverbs 13:15; 16:22; 19:11). But it does this by suggestion rather than quotation, inviting readers to make the connections for themselves as they are drawn into the story. This is perhaps because Esther tells its story from the perspective of weakness. The more we read the story and make the suggested connections to other parts of the Bible, the richer it becomes.

As we reflect on the book of Esther, we might consider some of the following questions.

- What does it mean to live for Jesus today from the position of weakness? What clues might Esther offer that will help us to do so?
- How can we embody the story of Jesus in our communal life and so commend it to our world without being explicit about it?
- How might people see something different about Christian community, even if they cannot explain it fully?
- How much do people need to know about God to begin to recognise his work in the world and among us?

FURTHER READING

Linda M. Day, *Esther*, Abingdon Press, 2005.

David G. Firth, *God Present but Unseen: The message of Esther*, IVP, 2010.

Karen H. Jobes, *Esther: The NIV Application Commentary*, Zondervan, 1999.

Debra Reid, *Esther: An introduction and commentary*, IVP, 2008.

Missional leadership

The church is no different from the rest of the world in its fascination with and desire for good leadership, yet, amid the noisy clamour for 'success', the biblical reality of leadership is demonstrated as something potentially less glamorous in worldly terms. Leadership is tough. It demands creativity, hospitality, spiritual anointing, timeliness, vision and courage. In the first week of these notes, we will investigate what characteristics and values we find in scripture that can inspire us to be world-changing, life-giving and disciple-making leaders.

Sports professionals often talk about 'reaching their potential', but this goal is not applicable only to the realm of sporting prowess. At the very core of our identity as human beings, we want to be liked, trusted and valued, to be noticed and considered competent, perhaps even to be compared favourably with other people.

In Christian leadership, too, comparisons are made. We may feel a need to prove that our sermons are more effective, our mission strategies reaping a bigger harvest, and our music more rousing for the audience than in other churches. Leadership is incredibly tough, and the sense of not reaching our potential (or not reaching God's expectations) can at times be suffocating.

There are all sorts of reasons why we may fail to reach our potential, including the pressures of life, the choices we make and even the location in which we live. Some of these factors are our own responsibility; others are external forces that are unpredictable and occasionally catastrophic.

Following Jesus does not inoculate us against these experiences. In the second week of notes, we look at some leadership lessons that have been learnt through the threat of persecution, the power of memory, the shadow of predecessors, conflict, lack of influence, and disciplined discipleship. We shall find that even in these more negative experiences and challenges, God's purposes are achieved. It is often true that leaders gain more by learning from mistakes and failure than through success.

Quotations are taken from the New International Version of the Bible.

1 Caring and creative leadership

Genesis 1:26–31

At the beginning of all things, God creates human beings and offers them an instruction. Even before they eat from the tree of the knowledge of good and evil and are banished from the garden of Eden, God asks humans to 'rule' over the earth and all living things on it (v. 28). The very first act of leadership for humankind, therefore, is to care for creation—to nurture the very fabric of life and to enable good stewardship of resources for the benefit of the whole earth.

This is a high calling indeed; the Creator invites the highlight of his creation, humankind, to live carefully and caringly with the earth. Made in God's own image, human beings are to continue to co-create in partnership with God. Leadership, then, is not primarily about high-flown theories of strategy or communication. Leadership is about carbon footprints, recycling of bottles, sustainable use of resources and access to clean water. The key to exercising leadership is to take seriously the beauty and potential of the whole of creation and to celebrate its diversity, provision and delicate balance.

In contrast with other creation mythologies of the ancient Near East, the biblical creation is a blessing, not a curse. God provides for his creation and enables it to flourish. Humankind is the pinnacle of creation, not the bane of it. God has a relationship with human beings and provides sustenance for them, rather than using them in forced labour. Thus, humans are called to be nurtured within this relationship, to worship their creator, to seek his provision and, in turn, to be nurturing toward others.

The story also suggests that leadership (and, arguably, the art of being human) involves being creative. The American professor Brene Brown, in her seminal book *The Gifts of Imperfection*, recognises that 'if we want to make meaning, we need to make art. Cook, write, draw, doodle, paint, scrapbook, take pictures, collage, knit, rebuild an engine, sculpt, dance, decorate, act, sing—it doesn't matter. As long as we're-creating, we're cultivating meaning.' The very act of creativity is an act of leadership that brings human beings into alignment with the heart of God's character.

2 Hospitable leadership

Acts 18:1–9, 18–19a

Paul's experience shows us all the traumas and difficulties of engaging in mission. Coming to the end of his second missionary journey, he has encountered opposition in Philippi, Thessalonica and Berea, and has met a rather cool reception in Athens. Now in Corinth, focusing his attention on preaching to his fellow Jews, his mission is proving difficult. Lonely, frustrated and tired, Paul finds solace in the company of two tentmakers, Aquila and Priscilla. When he is at his lowest ebb, he returns to the comfort of the trade he knows best.

Priscilla and Aquila are to become key leaders in the life of the church, travelling later with Paul from Corinth to Ephesus (vv. 18–19). Forced to be nomadic themselves, they know from their own experience the trauma of leaving home and having to start again, having been among the Jews expelled from Rome by the emperor Claudius (v. 2). They quickly open their home and their trade to Paul, offering him hospitality, solace and the opportunity to find his feet and his faith afresh. It is from this context that God then speaks to Paul, encouraging him not to keep quiet but to continue speaking out for the truth of the gospel (v. 9).

Leadership, then, can be about both giving and receiving hospitality. We often think of hospitality as offering a home to people or community groups, as Priscilla and Aquila offered a home to Paul, but leadership may also involve receiving the hospitality of others. Paul accepted the invitation to be known by them at a vulnerable and deep level, and to share their trade, craft and food. The result was encouragement, renewed strength and success for Paul and new opportunities for Priscilla and Aquila to be involved in mission.

This passage speaks of the need for leaders, like Priscilla and Aquila, to offer hospitality and to discern their own calling and missional vision. Significantly, however, it also challenges leaders to be courageous enough to receive the hospitality of those who will draw alongside and nurture them.

3 Anointed leadership

2 Kings 2:1–15

In the midst of change or transition, it can be difficult to see the potential in people and situations. Especially if it is unwelcome or enforced, change can be a paralysing experience as identity and hope are lost and the power of grief takes over. Changes in leadership, in particular, do not always bring out the best in people. When such problems arise, it is tempting to withdraw from a situation and retreat into a place of comfort and security, rather than press in to bring about God's intention for a place or people.

In today's passage, though, we see transition not as a threat but as an opportunity. Elijah is coming towards the end of his life, and he begins his final journey with a desire to find a solitary place. On three separate occasions, Elijah tells Elisha to leave him, and, on all three occasions, Elisha refuses. Firstly, then, leadership is about dogged determination, and especially a determination to finish well. Elijah is determined to finish his journey in the place where the Lord has sent him.

Equally, though, Elisha has no intention of leaving Elijah's side and vows to remain with him until the appointed hour. Elijah recognises, at last, that a good leader looks beyond the end of their own personal road. His relationship with Elisha is an opportunity to ensure that God's work continues and to offer a blessing on his own successor. Elisha shares this concern for a continuation of leadership, answering Elijah's final question, 'What can I do for you?' with a request for a double portion of his spirit. Elisha does not want property, a prayer, or even power for himself. He has seen the power of God at work and seeks to ensure that God's work will continue for future generations.

Significantly, Elisha's request is for something that Elijah, in fact, cannot give him—the anointing of the Spirit of God. Regardless of our personal desires and relationships, and however good are the plans and purposes we have put in place, anointed, Spirit-filled leadership remains the gift of God, not of human beings. Leadership is about seeking God's plans and purposes for a situation and working with the Spirit to see God's kingdom come on earth.

4 Timely leadership

When those in leadership are distanced from the people who are directly affected by their decisions, it is easy for them to bring in policies that are remote from the concerns of daily life. Esther learns to be a leader in just this situation. As a member of the king's court, she remains unaware of the suffering being endured by her family and friends. It is only when Mordecai comes as close to the city wall as he is allowed, in mourning clothes, that word reaches Esther of the plight of the Jews in the surrounding area. The hopes of the Jews are pinned on Esther's close proximity to the king, and, if she is to become a leader on their behalf, she needs to maintain a connection with them as well as with the powerful people whom she might influence.

It takes a lot of negotiation to persuade Esther that the time is right for her to approach the king and change public policy. She remains unsure, and tries to find excuses not to act (v. 11). Whether she likes it or not, however, Esther is in a position of power, influence and authority. She has the opportunity and the means to effect change on behalf of God's chosen people. She is the right person in the right place at the right time.

Mordecai brings the reality of her situation home: 'If you remain silent at this time, relief and deliverance for the Jews will arise from another place, but you and your father's family will perish. And who knows but that you have come to royal position for such a time as this?' (v. 14). Survival and self-preservation are good triggers for action. Leadership is often about recognising the opportune moment to act, and sometimes leaders need the help of other people, like Mordecai, to read the situation for them and to put issues into perspective.

Throughout this chapter, Esther maintains her composure and, eventually, she recognises that she has the power to change the world. Leadership requires great patience and preparation, prayerful watching and waiting, and then decisive action.

5 Visionary leadership

Nehemiah is a popular biblical character for study by those teaching and researching leadership credentials. Faced with the rubble of Jerusalem's ruined city walls, and knowing that it mirrors the overthrow of the entire Jewish nation, Nehemiah first takes a walk.

Leadership can start with simply going for a walk—seeing the world from a different perspective, understanding the source of the problem fully and then searching for a solution. We often expect solutions to come from boardroom tables or from behind desks in open-plan offices. In reality, though, how much more significant are the epiphanies that emerge during a sandwich break, in the shower, or as slumber descends at the end of the day! Nehemiah steps out on the broken wall and begins to sense a vision of what might be possible.

Then, 'Come, let us rebuild the wall,' declares Nehemiah as he sets forth the vision firmly (v. 17). The concept is communicated effectively: the wall will be rebuilt. Despite the pain and trauma of the past, there is work to do and a mission to carry out. Even in the face of opposition, Nehemiah does not engage deeply with the people who are standing in his way but, instead, continues to share the vision and encourage people to achieve it together.

Leadership involves communicating a vision in such a way that people begin to see their part in achieving it. In Nehemiah 3, we find a list of individuals who played their part in rebuilding the wall, strategically offering themselves to the success of the project. Leadership is not about doing everything oneself or expecting marvels from a small team. For Nehemiah, it meant encouraging the whole community to take responsibility for sections of the wall and to rebuild within their means. It is a startling picture of teamwork and obedience. Leadership offers a realistic overview of a task, shows how it may be achieved locally, and then celebrates achievements publicly and personally (note the details of names, places and relationships in chapter 3).

Vision brings people alive to the possibility of re-creation out of trauma and tragedy.

6 Courageous leadership

Joshua 1:1–9

The promised land stretches out before the Hebrew people as they march toward their newfound freedom. Their faith in the promises of God has been stretched to breaking point, and yet, even with their complaints, their drift into idol worship and the challenges of desert life, they have finally made it to the last obstacle, the River Jordan.

As they began to survey the land before them, the newly appointed leader, Joshua, must have realised the enormity of the task before him. To someone who had spied on the residents of the promised land and then seen God's fulfilment of his promises, the prospect of leadership must have been both exciting and overwhelming. It would be no surprise if, in the midst of these turbulent emotions, Joshua needed to be reminded of God's presence with him.

In times of transition and uncertainty, as an old order of power dissolves and new ideas are needed for a new context, Joshua offers a vision of courageous and strategic leadership. He hears the word of God spoken to him and, through this discernment, sets the hearts of his family and the Hebrew people in the direction of God's purposes for them—in a particular place and time, and with specific obstacles ahead. Joshua's clear thinking, courage and competence are not merely human skills that he has developed under expert tutelage. Joshua's strength is found in the Lord God, through whom, as Joshua's name ('the Lord saves') suggests, God's people will find their salvation.

To this relatively inexperienced man, God speaks of land and settlement and home. He speaks Joshua into leadership, encouraging him: be strong and courageous! Do not give in to the negative thoughts raging through your head. Use your nerves to be exceptional, not cowardly. Your calling is to bring a vision of God's people settling in this land of milk and honey. You are capable. This is your time and your moment. Be strong and courageous! Take heart. You are not alone.

As we can read in the subsequent chapters, Joshua goes on to lead with audacious courage, developing his own team of adventurous leaders with whom he entrusts the very survival of a nation.

Guidelines

Leadership can bring transformation into a situation. Spiritual leadership, at its best, can release great creativity, enthusiasm and excitement. History is marked by people who, through their prayerful engagement with scripture and their willingness to be deeply affected by situations in need of transformation, have worked to change public policy, worldviews and opinions. The church has the potential to be a transformative group of people, engaged in public life and personal devotion in a wide variety of ways. Without appropriate, engaged, prophetic leadership, however, it can also be a place of pressure, exhaustion and apathy.

Look back over the week's studies and consider these questions:

- How might you celebrate your creativity today, recalling that you are made in the image of a creative, caring and re-creative God who seeks to see you flourish?
- From whom do you need to receive hospitality today? What challenges does their invitation present for you?
- What opportunities do you see in the changing world around you? What might God's anointing look like in these situations?
- Where have you been the right (or wrong) person at the right time? How do you stay alert to prayerful action today, 'for such a time as this'?
- Where can you find reflective space, renewed vision and realistic overviews of your situation today?
- Where do you need to be more courageous, adventurous and audacious in your leadership and discipleship?

1 Persecuted leadership

Acts 9:10–19

Saul was a renowned Jewish leader, commanding fear among the growing Christian community, often being responsible for the persecution, capture and martyrdom of the followers of 'the Way'. His journey to Damascus should not have been any different from any other. It was likely that news had spread to the Christian community there about Saul's approach, and they would have been frightened for their lives. One among them was Ananias. He knew of Saul's behaviour and had been alerted to Saul's plan to persecute and capture more followers of Jesus on this trip.

However, as is so often the case, God had other plans. Saul encountered Jesus on the main road, becoming physically blind, and Ananias, a faithful leader of the church, was called by God to welcome Saul into the Christian community. Leadership often means being faithful to God's calling, even if it sounds like the worst possible option.

Despite his initial eagerness to follow wherever God might lead ('Yes, Lord', v. 10), once the plan is revealed, Ananias is less than enthusiastic. His mind starts to reel with all the 'What if...?' scenarios that present themselves. What if it is a trick, and Saul is pretending to be something he is not? What if this is not really God speaking at all?

In an act of obedient leadership, however, Ananias goes to meet Saul, addressing him with the respectful and equitable greeting, 'Brother Saul'. Leadership, especially in uncertain times, is about stepping into the unknown with grace, which in turn brings respect and transformation. Ananias begins to model for Paul what it might mean for him to be accepted into a Jewish Christian environment, to be nurtured and served by the very people he has sought to attack.

In our world, so often marked by attack, enmity and intolerance, Ananias' leadership here shows us an alternative. By stepping into the unknown to offer grace and equality, trusting in God's plan, Ananias is enabled to build community, not barriers.

2 Abundant leadership

Genesis 43:17–34

This is an emotional moment for Joseph. He was once sold into slavery because he was just a little too arrogant and dangerous in the eyes of his brothers. Then he was wrongly accused of a crime and thrown into jail. There, he took the opportunity to speak into other people's lives and saw his prophecies come to reality, eventually risking his own Hebrew identity in order to serve an Egyptian ruler and keep a nation alive. However, Joseph is a leader who is not defined by the experiences of his past. Instead, he has worked to build relationships with Pharaoh, his fellow prisoners and his siblings, and to seek reconciliation.

For Joseph, this encounter with his brothers is an opportunity to meet the needs of people he cares deeply about. He is not afraid to be guided by his own gut reactions in the situation, withdrawing from the crowd until he regains his emotional composure (v. 30). Leadership, at this moment in Joseph's life, means being prepared to break with convention, to eat with people thought to be unclean, and to serve the brothers who, as yet, do not recognise him. Joseph is neither defined by the memory of the pain his brothers caused him nor motivated to take revenge. Rather, he demonstrates his knowledge to them by sitting them in age order and making sure that they all have enough to eat and drink.

Leadership can often involve a gracious and generous act, surprising those who feel they are being victimised or threatened by a situation or system. It can be an act of emotion, as leadership today requires sensitivity not only to the needs of the other but also to the needs of the self. Leadership is about physically and metaphorically sitting alongside those who should be, or consider themselves to be, our enemies, breaking with conventions and starting to rebuild relationships. Leadership is also about recognising the physical needs of those in our care and responding to their physical as well as their deeper psychological and spiritual needs.

3 Succession planning

1 Kings 14:21–31

It is always difficult stepping into the shoes of a powerful and successful predecessor like Solomon, who not only built the temple but also brought great wealth and success to the Israelites. Often, the final mark of effective leadership is the ability to hand over responsibility smoothly to the next generation.

Rehoboam is tasked with being the next generation of leadership for the kingdom of Judah, yet this short passage marks the whole of his reign. Although he is a king by birthright, we soon learn that he has not been mentored well and thus fails to keep his people in line with God's precepts. Instead, the people are seduced by pluralistic religious ideologies and practices, and they fall away from God. Not only that, but the nation also begins to lose its material assets, as it comes under almost constant attack from its neighbours.

Rehoboam's 17-year reign is reduced to eleven verses of scripture. His whole legacy is marked by conflict, loss, and the repeated assertion that he is, after all, his mother's son (vv. 21, 31).

Succession in leadership is always difficult to orchestrate, and can be even more difficult to receive. Rehoboam obviously fails to be a good leader, spending the last years of his life watching the sharp decline of his father's kingdom. In the midst of tensions and conflict, and with the weight of expectation upon him, Rehoboam's position is one that might evoke our sympathy. Perhaps, however, the blame for the trauma of his reign should not be laid solely at his door: the transition would have been aided by better examples from Solomon and other neighbouring leaders.

Leadership is about bringing the next generation into their own vocation, enabling them to succeed without being overshadowed by the power of memory or the burden of expectation. It is also about being courageous enough to trust that each individual leader has the gifts, graces and skills to be themselves, and not to expect them to fit into the mould of another person.

4 Collaborative leadership

Acts 11:25–30

As opportunities for mission and ministry grow, so too does the need for equipped and gifted leaders to take on the work.

The church in Antioch was growing, especially among the Gentiles. Barnabas recognised that there was a need for more leadership, so he prayerfully sought out the person who he believed had the skills and gifts to work in that situation. Barnabas did not look for the 'whole package' (Saul was not, at this stage, fully developed in his ministry) but, instead, took the risk of working with someone with potential. Leadership, therefore, involves enabling other people to join a team and to participate as fully as possible in it.

It is also significant that Barnabas did not work with just anyone in the immediate vicinity. Rather, he searched Saul out. Barnabas was looking specifically for someone who could minister to the mixed congregation in Antioch, who could speak into that situation with authority, inspiring respect.

This was not a quick fix or a simple solution to the missional challenge of Antioch. Barnabas was already heavily invested in ministry in the city, but he took the time to invest in Saul's leadership. Barnabas and Saul spent a whole year together in mission in that context (v. 26), speaking with the people and facing up to the challenges that presented themselves. Leadership is a long-haul vocation, and collaborative or team leadership can become especially difficult at times. It takes time to develop, and it has to be intentional in order to be effective. Conflict can arise, and differences of opinion can lead quickly to irreconcilable divisions and broken relationships. Not even Paul and Barnabus were immune to this danger, as we discover later, in Acts 15:36–41.

Leadership involves collaboration and challenge, even at the risk of conflict. Leaders must also recognise that experience is not always required in a given situation. Collaboration can take us out of our comfort zones and extend our worldview. It also needs time to grow and flourish.

5 Influencial leadership

Acts 19:23–34

Leadership expert John Maxwell says, 'Leadership is influence.' Influence can involve coercion, ignorance and alienation, as leadership is almost always about the use of power among a group of people. Used well, however, power need not be destructive or oppressive. Good leadership requires integrity and an understanding of what is going on in a locality or community.

In Acts 19, Ephesus is on the brink of collapse. A riot has broken out over a few pieces of silver, but underlying the incident is a fear that the economic stability of local businesses may be threatened if the new worldview of Christianity takes hold. What began as a debate about trinkets escalates quickly and dangerously, to become a riot over religious ideology and practice. The whole city falls into disarray, committed to protecting the divinity of the goddess Artemis. The theatre is full of people and there is utter confusion, with many of the rioters not really knowing what they are protesting about (v. 32).

Influential leaders should notice when confusion has taken over and should have the wherewithal to speak into the heart of the situation. Instead, in Ephesus, Alexander is pushed forward. He is a silversmith (possibly the metalworker mentioned by Paul in 2 Timothy 4:14), so he is expected to be able to speak to the crowd about silver and statues and jewellery. His fellow Jews fail to recognise, though, that Alexander has no influence with the crowd. To them, he is a Jew who represents the threat that they are opposing—the challenge to the worship of Artemis. As far as they are concerned, Alexander has no integrity, and the crowd begin a chant that lasts for two hours.

It is only the city clerk, the political governor, who is able to bring silence and calm the riot. His influence stems from the law, offering a recognised process to those who feel threatened. Legal power and authority are wielded, and the people are dismissed. This is not the kind of influence that either side in the riot expected to prevail. However, it demonstrates the difference between influential leadership that knows the context and can speak into it and leadership that is well-meaning and well-mannered but ultimately ignorant and powerless.

6 Disciplined leadership

Acts 2:42–47

Leadership can be a lonely experience at times, isolating individuals rather than enabling them to flourish in community. The challenge for leaders is to find ways to exercise sustainable practices and characteristics which enable them to face and learn from the complexities, riots and challenges of everyday life, even deepening their faith in the process.

At the cornerstone of the early church were several communal practices, which enabled the leadership of the apostles to be sustained in the midst of transition and persecution. Together, the disciples were devoted to their community, biblical teaching, prayer and Communion. They wanted to make sure that they had the right foundations and the right relationships, both with each other and with God.

The single main priority for Christian leaders, therefore, is to maintain their personal devotion to Jesus. Leadership is first and foremost about discipleship, spending time reading scripture, praying and being resourced for the ministry and the context to which we are called. The disciples recognised that they needed to be taught, just as much as they themselves taught others. They sought out opportunities to wrestle with key themes and ideas, and to come to a common mind about issues of dogma, doctrine and practice.

Leadership is also a corporate exercise. Fellowship was at the heart of the disciplines of the early church. In our culture, which prizes individuality and strong personality, it can be countercultural to think of leadership as a shared experience. Out of our personal devotion to God and corporate responsibility to each other, however, flows the transformation of the world. It is in the context of community that prayers are answered, miracles witnessed and testimony offered. Then church growth becomes a living reality,

Leadership is a Spirit-inspired, Christ-centred, community-focused, missional vocation. We therefore have a high calling to a life of discipleship and disciplines by which our leadership can be underpinned and sustained.

Guidelines

In our society, leadership can go hand in hand with celebrity, and power can be used to abuse rather than to release people. It is easy for us to covet the influence that comes with leadership. Its reach can be intoxicating, and we can be seduced by its vanity.

However, the Bible consistently tells stories of imperfect people trying their best to seek out God's will for a community, discern the Spirit at work in their midst and act accordingly. In the midst of these imperfect people and situations, God continues to be at work.

At its heart, Christian leadership is about living holy lives—prayerful, discerning, communal and Christ centred. As we have seen, leadership need not be limited by expectations or memories, persecution or fear. It might be discovered in authentic engagement with people, getting to grips with context, and sharing leadership opportunities with unlikely candidates. Leadership vocation might be found in questions and long conversations over mugs of coffee. Vision may be heard on the lips of the marginalised and those who have little power or influence in the world's eyes.

The challenge for leaders, then, is to be of God's heart, to take notice, to take risks, to adventure in collaboration with others, to be creative and, ultimately, to change the world.

Looking back over the week, consider the following questions.

- Where might you need to step into the unknown and begin to lead with grace, equality and trust? Are any 'What ifs' stopping you from reaching your potential?
- How can you be more generous with your time and your assets? When might you need to act on instinct?
- What is your leadership succession plan? In what situations do you need to stand your ground, rather than cave in to expectations placed upon you by other people?
- Where have you experienced creative collaborative leadership? Who might you be able to search out and collaborate with now?
- How do you use power and influence? How might you gain greater credibility and influence in your locality?
- What practices of discipleship do you need to be reminded of, to sustain you in your leadership?

Acts 8:26—16:40

This section of Acts sees the most radical changes in the believing community's life, as the Jewish believers gradually realise that God is drawing them out to embrace and include Gentiles. The movement begins with the half-bred Samaritans (8:4–25) and develops through a God-fearing Ethiopian eununch (8:26–40), God's call of Saul of Tarsus (9:1–30), who will be 'the apostle to the Gentiles', the great breakthrough of Peter's encounter with the Roman centurion Cornelius (10:1—11:18), and on into the formation of the first mixed Jewish/Gentile church in Syrian Antioch (11:19–26).

This expansion creates controversy, and we can see the flavour and temperature of that controversy in Paul's letter to the Galatians, written while much of this activity was going on. There Paul attacks Jewish believers who want to require Gentile believers to keep the Jewish law and submit to circumcision: he insists that faith in Jesus is the only 'entry requirement' that the Christian community should have. You might like to read Galatians through at a sitting to get a sense of how important this issue was to Paul.

We live long after this controversy has been resolved, and the division lines in our Christian communities today are different. Yet the story has much to say to us about the nature of the church and the need to be clear on what is central and what is secondary. Look for these issues as you read through Acts 8—16, and ask God, as you read, to help you recognise how to engage with the sharp end of controversies that unite and divide Christians today.

For the believers during this period, God's love for the whole ethnically diverse world became the central and dominant theme. John 3:16, 'For God so loved *the world*…' might be the motto of this section of Acts.

Quotations are taken from the New Revised Standard Version.

20–26 July

1 Philip's appointment with the Ethiopian

Acts 8:26–40

The gospel's journey 'to the ends of the earth' (Acts 1:8) continues through Philip, as God's messenger, an angel, directs him to go to the middle of nowhere (v. 26). Just at the right time, a remarkable man comes along: Luke calls him only 'the eunuch' (vv. 27, 34, 38, 39), but he has a fourfold identity (vv. 27–28). He comes from modern Sudan, so he is dark-skinned ('Ethiopian' in Greek means 'burnt-face'): racism by skin colour was uncommon in the ancient world. He is powerful, as the finance minister of the Ethiopian queen. He is a eunuch, castrated to serve a queen, with an ambiguous gender status. Significantly, he is spiritually hungry: he has been to Jerusalem hoping to worship—a journey of some 1300 miles. However, Luke implies that he has come away disappointed, for eunuchs could not take part in Israel's worship (Deuteronomy 23:1). Nevertheless, he is persistent, for he is reading the book of Isaiah, possibly purchased in Jerusalem. Only a wealthy person could afford an expensive manuscript, which underlines his seriousness in seeking God.

To this man, God sends Philip and, by the Spirit, encourages Philip to speak to him (v. 29). Philip hears the man reading Isaiah (v. 30): all reading in ancient times was done aloud. The eunuch's 'chariot' was an ox-cart, the vehicle of a civil (rather than military) official, so Philip would have been able to keep up with it by jogging gently. Philip is wise enough to ask this powerful man a question to engage his interest (v. 30), and this opens the way for Philip to explain about Jesus: the section of Isaiah that the eunuch is reading is about the 'suffering servant' (53:7–8), whom Christians saw as foreshadowing Jesus' suffering and death. Perhaps Philip read on to Isaiah 56:3–8, which promises God's welcome to eunuchs in coming times: that passage would certainly have resonated with the Ethiopian.

Given the eunuch's experience of exclusion in Jerusalem, he asks whether anything prevents him from being baptised (v. 36), and Philip is able to assure him that the gospel includes him. Philip baptises him (v. 38), so he rejoices (v. 39). Then, God who has brought them together for a key moment takes each of them on to the next part of their lives. That's a divine appointment!

2 Saul of Tarsus meets the exalted Jesus

Acts 9:1–31

Saul of Tarsus is remarkably transformed from a persecutor of believers to an apostle and evangelist—and it is entirely the work of the exalted Jesus.

Jesus is not absent from the stage of history now that he is in heaven (1:9–11): he is actively engaged, ruling *from* heaven. Follow the stages as Saul's life and the life of Jesus become intertwined: these stages reflect Luke's teaching on Christian conversion.

Firstly, Saul is satisfied with his life as a Pharisee: his devotion to Jewish law and lifestyle is so great that he persecutes Jesus' followers (vv. 1–2). They worship a crucified Messiah—a contradiction in terms. Saul's faith is turned into action as he travels to Damascus (in Syria) to arrest the followers of Jesus. Saul shows no sign of doubt about his purpose and underlying beliefs here, beliefs that he summarises later in Philippians 3:4b–6. Jesus, amazingly, meets this opponent and greets him by name (v. 4).

Secondly, Saul is humbled by meeting Jesus: he falls down and recognises Jesus' authority as 'Lord' (vv. 4–5). He learns that he has been attacking Jesus himself by attacking his people (v. 5b). This signals that Jesus is now present where his people are present, all over the world. Jesus is truly Lord of *all* (see 10:36). Saul's humbling continues as Jesus keeps him in suspense about what will happen next: Saul is simply to go to Damascus and await directions (v. 6).

Thirdly, from the heavenly perspective, Jesus has prepared the way, calling Ananias to go to Saul (vv. 11–12). Ananias cannot quite believe that his Lord would be so foolish, and says so (vv. 13–14), but Jesus reassures him (vv. 15–16). This scene will be echoed when Peter argues with the Lord about eating unclean animals (10:9–16). Acts is far from being a story of believers who cooperate with God promptly: God-in-Jesus takes the initiative, often dragging his people kicking and screaming behind.

Finally, when Saul is healed and baptised, Jesus' Sprit empowers him for his new role (v. 17; see 2:38) when Ananias shares what Jesus has said to him (vv. 15–16). At last, Saul responds with obedience: he has been humbled and now thinks of himself rightly (see Romans 3) as one who can help others respond to the gospel. His zeal is redirected to testifying publicly to Jesus (vv. 19b–21), rather than seeking to destroy the church.

3 The gradual conversion of Peter (1)

Acts 9:43—10:23a

Peter's encounter with God here results in the household of Cornelius, a Roman centurion, coming to faith in Jesus. Luke tells this story partly through Cornelius' eyes, highlighting this Gentile's conversion to Jesus, and partly through Peter's eyes. We shall focus on *Peter's* conversion, for he is God's key agent in drawing Cornelius to Jesus. Peter's radical change will be vital in enabling the believing community also to change, to admit people to the church who are not Jewish. Luke tells the story three times (here, in 11:1–18 and, briefly, in 15:7–9) to show its importance for the gospel.

Peter is already beginning to change at the start of this story, for he is staying in the home of Simon the tanner (9:43). Tanning is an unclean trade for Jews, so staying in such a place carries the risk of ritual pollution—the kind associated with eating Gentile food or visiting Gentile homes.

Yet, when Peter sees a large sheet full of animals, birds and reptiles (vv. 11–12), a mix of creatures that Jews consider ritually clean and unclean, he refuses to obey the voice that says, 'Kill and eat' (vv. 13–14). The voice's explanation, 'What God has made clean, you must not call profane' (v. 15), doesn't make things clearer, and nor does the threefold repetition of the vision (v. 16). However, through this vision God prepares Peter to recognise that Gentile *people* are not unclean: the meaning of the vision is not about animals.

Meanwhile, an angel goes to Cornelius, for God is seeking Cornelius as much as Cornelius is seeking God (vv. 2, 4). When the angel tells Cornelius to call for Peter, this pagan (by contrast with Peter the believer) is quick to respond. Cornelius sends his people to fetch Peter from Joppa, most of a day's journey away (vv. 3, 9). Even as they approach, Peter is seeing his vision: God's timing is immaculate, just as it was in the encounter between Philip and the Ethiopian.

At last, Peter begins to understand, for the Spirit prompts him to receive the three visitors 'without hesitation' (v. 20), overcoming his natural Jewish concern at welcoming pagan, ritually unclean Gentiles. Peter now starts moving with God, taking the first steps. He invites the visitors to stay—and that involves eating with unclean Gentiles (v. 23a).

4 The gradual conversion of Peter (2)

Acts 10:23b–48

Peter, like many of us, is slow to catch on that God wants real and radical change. It's easy for our church life today to be the same as it was years ago, to have all the order of a graveyard rather than the riotous life of a meadow of wild flowers. We can be tempted to think and act as if our unchanging and reliable God wants everything to stay the same. So how does Peter continue to change in this story?

First, he is honest about his assumptions and the place he has reached on his journey with God. When he meets the crowd that Cornelius has assembled, he tells them how surprised he is to be there: he has learned that God does not regard people as 'profane or unclean' (v. 28), evidently as a result of reflecting on his vision and God's instruction to welcome Cornelius' messengers.

Second, he asks a question that allows Cornelius to tell his story and express his own desire to know God (v. 29). Jesus did the same sort of thing brilliantly (see Luke 18:41), inviting people to speak honestly about themselves—and, by the Spirit, Peter is equipped to follow his example.

Third, Peter responds to Cornelius' story of the angel's visit by making connections that show him more of what God is doing: God is not biased for or against one part of humanity, but welcomes and loves all who seek him (vv. 34–35). Without Cornelius' testimony, Peter might not have made this connection fully. Peter goes on to explain the story of Jesus to Cornelius (vv. 36–43). This Roman's prior experience of God is insufficient alone. The story of Jesus needs to be told to bring it to completion and to lead Cornelius to a full knowledge of God-in-Jesus.

Finally, when God acts further, by sending the Spirit to fall on the group, the final link in the chain is clear to Peter. He must baptise these people, for God has welcomed them and given them the Spirit, just as he did to the original believers at Pentecost (2:4). Now, Peter is willing not only to have Gentiles in his home but also to stay with Gentiles in theirs, sharing meals with people he formerly regarded as unclean (v. 48b).

5 Barnabas: a key player

Acts 11:19–30

Barnabas is one of the stars of the earliest church, but he is not a man in the spotlight. We first met him giving generously to the believing community (4:36–37) and then helping Saul of Tarsus to be accepted by the Jerusalem believers (9:27). Now comes perhaps Barnabas' most important single contribution to the church's establishment and growth: he has the wisdom to draw Saul into the first mixed Jewish–Gentile believing group, in Antioch.

Even though the Jewish church in Jerusalem has reluctantly recognised that God welcomes 'even' Gentiles (11:18), the scattered believers are still speaking about Jesus only to Jewish people (v. 19). However, some from Cyprus and north Africa (Cyrene) arrive in Antioch (in modern Syria) and start to proclaim Jesus to Gentiles ('Hellenists', v. 20), with success. These believers are among those driven out of Jerusalem by persecution (8:1), so this development may be happening around the same time as Peter's encounter with Cornelius. If so, God is using a two-pronged approach to reaching beyond the Jewish community.

The Jerusalem church gives Barnabas the job of checking things out in Antioch (v. 22). Are these Gentiles genuinely trusting in Israel's God as now known in Jesus? Barnabas is perfect for the role. His approach is to look for what God is doing and to work with it, rather than adopting a box-ticking approach that requires the new Antioch believers to meet preconditions. What he sees is God's generous love ('grace', v. 23) at work, and he is delighted.

Barnabas goes further, however, for he sees the need for instruction and growth among the new believers in Antioch. He provides what he can himself (v. 23b), but he knows that there is someone who can give better assistance—Saul. Barnabas makes the considerable journey of some 185 miles (285 km) overland to Tarsus to find Saul and persuade him to come to Antioch to help the new community (vv. 25–26).

The fruit of this teaching ministry comes quickly, as Agabus warns of a forthcoming famine (v. 28). The group in Antioch responds generously: God's grace, which Barnabas recognised (v. 25), is worked out in their grace toward the Jewish Christians of Judea (v. 29). Instruction received leads to growth in grace.

6 God is honoured in death and in deliverance

Acts 12:1–24

Believers follow Jesus in the way of his cross and resurrection. That road entails pain (for it is the way of the cross), but the pain leads to glory (for it is also the way of resurrection). Within God's sovereign purposes, Christians sometimes suffer and die at the hands of those who oppose the gospel: Acts is realistic about this fact and does not hide James' execution at Herod's hands (v. 2). Suffering is not the whole story, though, for God can and does act in remarkable ways to protect and prosper his people in the midst of painful times. Here we see two examples of divine deliverance: Peter's release from prison and Herod's death.

Peter's release is a striking example both of God's saving intervention and of the believers' own engagement with God in the process. As Peter sits imprisoned, he is secure enough in God's hands to sleep amid this dangerous situation: Herod plans to 'bring him out' (v. 4) to have him tried and executed publicly. Indeed, Peter sleeps so soundly that the angel has to strike him to wake him (v. 7: NRSV's 'tapped' is too weak). Even then, Peter thinks he is dreaming as his chains fall off and they walk past two Roman guards and through the iron city gate (vv. 8–10). Peter cannot quite believe that God is releasing him.

The believers cannot believe it either, for when Rhonda, the servant, goes to tell the church prayer meeting that Peter, whom they are praying for (vv. 5, 12), is at the gate, they think it's impossible, and it must be his angel (v. 15; some Jews believed that godly people became angels when they died: compare Mark 12:25)! Peter has to keep hammering at the gate until they let him in (v. 16): sometimes God's actions in delivering his people seem too good to be true, and our only response can be thanksgiving.

Herod also cannot believe that God is as he truly is, and he accepts the kind of acclamation that is due to God alone (vv. 22–23). We can see a strong contrast here between Peter, who knows that he is merely human and refused divine honours when they were offered to him (10:25–26), and Herod, who wrongly accepts such honours and is struck down by God.

Guidelines

The earliest Christians saw great developments over a relatively short period: Acts 8:26—12:24 covers about ten years. Luke's 'edited highlights' focus on key episodes, so we might be misled into thinking that life in the early churches was remarkable all the time. However, Luke records these particular stories precisely because they were hinge-points, significant for the development and growth of God's work. Alongside these remarkable events went the quiet faithfulness of believers who lived and witnessed to their faith. Thus, unnamed believers planted the church in Antioch (8:4; 11:19–21). Philip disappears from view after his outstanding experiences of mission in Samaria and with the Ethiopian eunuch (8:40), and we only meet him again years later in Caesarea (21:8–9). Barnabas and Saul taught the Antioch believers for a whole year (11:26).

It is tempting to wish for our lives to be full of the remarkable rather than the ordinary, but this section of Acts invites us to see both as important. God can be and is at work in the ordinary, as people are drawn to faith by the steady witness of the believing community. God can be and is at work in the remarkable, and such events can be turning points for the development and growth of churches. Both are important, and the key is to look for what God is doing. This approach became a feature of the early believers' decision-making at the Jerusalem meeting (15:1–35), but it was already seen as vital.

Luke encourages us to rejoice that God is at work and to reflect on our lives, individually and as churches, asking the question, 'What is God doing here?' It's easy, in the midst of busy church life, to fail to ask that question—but to fail to ask it is to close our eyes to the most important things that are happening.

1 Recognising God's call

Acts 13:1–12

We puzzle over God's call. We wonder what God's call for our lives is, and how we will recognise it. It affects big life-changing decisions and smaller, day-to-day decisions. Here, God's call to Barnabas and Saul takes shape slowly.

Barnabas and Saul are involved in the church at Syrian Antioch, where Barnabas brought Saul to help with teaching a new group of believers (11:20–26). By now, there is a group of five who lead the church—and a very mixed group it is (v. 1). Simeon is dark-skinned (as shown by the name 'Niger'), and thus from Africa. Lucius is also African, from the coast of modern Libya. Manaen is an aristocrat, having grown up with Herod Antipas, the ruler of Galilee during Jesus' ministry. Barnabas is from a Jewish Levite family (4:36), and Saul comes from a Jewish Pharisaic background of persecuting the church. This is a group brought together only through shared faith in Jesus, and it is significant that three of them are willing for Barnabas and Saul to leave when God calls them away. There will be a cost for those who remain, in terms of a greater responsibility for leadership.

It is as the church seeks God seriously (worshipping and fasting, v. 2) that God speaks. To know God's will, we need to spend time growing to know him better. 'The Holy Spirit said' (v. 2) suggests that a church member spoke a prophetic word (see 21:11). However, the message is rather vague: Barnabas and Saul are not told specifically where to go, but only that they are called to the work God has for them. Luke suggests that Saul, at least, already knows that this work will involve sharing the gospel with Gentiles (see 9:15).

The phrasing in verse 3 suggests a further period of prayer and fasting before Barnabas and Saul are commissioned by laying on of hands and prayer. The believers reflect on and pray about the prophetic word and test it (see 1 Corinthians 14:29; 1 Thessalonians 5:19–21), concluding that this is indeed God's purpose.

So where to go? Without specific direction, they go first to Barnabas' home, Cyprus (v. 4; see 4:36), and begin the work of sharing the gospel which is to take them a long way over the years to come.

2 Engaging with Jewish people in ministry

Acts 13:13–52

What was the early Christians' message? Luke presents a 'set piece' by Paul (note the change of name at this point), speaking in the synagogue in

27 July–2 August

Pisidian Antioch (in the south of modern Turkey). Paul considered it vital to show his Jewish hearers that Jesus fulfilled scriptural hopes and prophecies, so this story is peppered with references to the Old Testament.

First, Paul summarises Israel's history, from the time when God delivered them from Egypt and brought them into the promised land (vv. 17–20), to the climactic point of David's kingship (v. 22). Jesus, he says, is Israel's true king, a royal descendant of David, Israel's greatest king and the fulfilment of the hopes of Israel.

Second, Paul interprets Jesus' death and resurrection through the lens of scripture. Jewish people were expecting a Messiah who would live and triumph over his enemies, so it was crucial for Christians to show that Jesus' death and resurrection were God's plan, prepared for in scripture. Paul uses scriptural texts to do this, quoting Psalm 2:7 (v. 33; see Hebrews 1:5; 5:5), Psalm 16:10 (v. 35; see 2:27) and Isaiah 55:3 (v. 34; see Hebrews 13:20)—an approach frequently used in early Christian apologetics among Jewish people.

Third, Paul cites scripture to warn of the danger of rejecting Jesus (v. 41; Habakkuk 1:5). To receive the gospel is to be set free from sins (v. 39); to reject Jesus is to face God's rejection.

Finally, when some Jewish people oppose Paul and Barnabas as they prepare to speak to a wide range of people, including Gentiles, the pair quote scripture to justify their mission among the Gentiles. Pointing to the Servant in Isaiah, they interpret his role as a light to Gentiles (v. 47; Isaiah 49:6) as being about Jesus' and his people's role in reaching beyond the bounds of Israel to the whole world.

To read Acts (or other parts of the New Testament) without seeing the way that Old Testament scripture is interpreted by the believers is to miss something vital. God's purposes for the world did not begin with Jesus but flow from Israel's history. Jesus' life, death, resurrection and exaltation are rightly understood when seen though this lens. To be a Christian reader of scripture is to be one who is immersed in the whole Bible, both Old and New Testaments.

3 Engaging with pagans in gospel ministry

Acts 14:8–20

Being misunderstood is frustrating, and this is Barnabas and Paul's experience in Lystra, a Roman colony in Lycaonia, a rural region in the mid-south of modern Turkey. The locals have a legend that the gods Zeus and Hermes once visited but were rejected, with dire consequences for the town, so when Paul commands a man lame from birth to walk (vv. 8–10), they are not going to make the same mistake twice. The priest of Zeus becomes involved, and Barnabas and Paul face a huge misunderstanding of their identity and message (vv. 11–13). It also takes them some time to realise what is going on, because the people are speaking Lycaonian (v. 11)—a local language, perhaps descended from the Hittite language.

What should they do in this situation? Telling the people just to stop will not be enough: they need to know who Barnabas and Paul really are and whom they serve. This is a new situation, for until now Paul has spoken to Jewish people or sympathetic Gentiles, people with a basic knowledge about God from scripture. Here, Paul and Barnabas are speaking to pagans whose assumptions about the gods are completely different, so they have to find a different starting point for their message.

They begin with God as creator (v. 15). Rather than being an idol made by humans, the true God has made the world; he is the living God, not a lifeless statue or an absentee god living it up on Mount Olympus. This God's kindness is seen in his provision of people's needs (v. 17). So Paul appeals to the Lystrans' inbuilt sense of gratitude for food—a sense that most people in most times and places share—and seeks to build on it. Paul begins where people are, and finds a point of contact that can offer a bridge to the full gospel message of Jesus.

True gospel ministry is like this encounter: as we engage with people and share the message of Jesus, we will meet misunderstanding and we will need to seek points of contact. This is challenging but indispensable, for God has entered our world as one of us, to enable us to meet him.

4 Which way now?

Acts 15:1–35

Some decisions are forks in the road, moments when the choice of direction changes life for ever. The Jerusalem meeting is such a moment, when the believing community's decision will change the church permanently.

The issue is the status of believers who follow Jesus without being Jewish, either by birth or by conversion (v. 3). Some within the predominantly Jewish believing community consider that following Jesus is so much a Jewish matter that these Gentiles must become Jewish: the men must be circumcised and they must all keep the Jewish law (vv. 1, 5). Others, represented by Paul and Barnabas (v. 2), believe that God welcomes Gentiles on the same basis as Jews—that is, only through faith in Jesus—so nothing else is necessary. Paul's letter to the Galatians (probably written shortly before this meeting took place) reflects the controversy; there, Paul insists that faith in Jesus is the crucial requirement for belonging to God, not circumcision or law-keeping (see Galatians 2:15–16; 3:6–13; 5:2–6).

The Jerusalem meeting rightly focuses on what God wants. Peter recalls his surprising encounter with Cornelius (vv. 6–11; 10:1–48) and stresses God's actions: 'God made a choice… God testified to them by giving them the Holy Spirit… He has made no distinction between them and us… Why are you putting God to the test?' Then Barnabas and Paul speak of what God has done among the Gentiles (v. 12). James, summing up, focuses on testimony from Peter to God's actions and interprets scripture (vv. 16–17, citing Amos 9:11–12 and echoing words from Hosea 3:5; Jeremiah 12:15–16; Isaiah 45:21) to show that God's intention is to draw Gentiles to himself. James' blending of several Old Testament passages (some based on Greek translation rather than the Hebrew from which our translations are made) is similar to the practice of rabbinic writings (written down from around AD200, but probably reflecting what happened in the first century).

The outcome is that Gentiles are not required to be circumcised or to keep the whole law. All that is required is that they avoid anything associated with idolatry (for each of the items in verses 20 and 29 is linked with idol worship), which was the great temptation for Gentiles and the great fear of the Jewish people.

The threat to the gospel's universal appeal at this time came from a temptation to focus on secondary issues at the cost of the primary one—God's acceptance of people through faith in Jesus alone. It's easy to major on minors: the church's constant challenge is to keep the main thing as the main thing!

5 Reaching out further to Jewish people

Acts 16:1–10

After Paul's robust insistence that Gentile believers must not be circumcised, supported by the Jerusalem meeting (15:19–29), it is very surprising that he then circumcises Timothy (v. 3). What could he have been thinking?

Behind Paul's action lies his passionate concern for the gospel of Jesus to be heard and believed by all kinds of people: he wants nothing to get in the way of that. He is prepared to adapt and be flexible about many secondary issues in order to enable the gospel to be heard. As he himself writes in 1 Corinthians 9:19–23, Paul is a Jew to Jews, a lawless Gentile to Gentiles, and so on. If it will help Jewish people to hear and respond to Jesus, he is willing to circumcise the mixed-race Timothy, to remove a potential barrier to ministry in the Jewish synagogues.

Paul does not think that circumcision is wrong for Jewish people: he insists that it is not to be required for Gentile believers in Jesus, and he will not allow any such requirement for a moment. In order to open the door for the gospel to be heard among Jews, however, he is prepared to circumcise Timothy, who becomes one of his key travelling companions and lieutenants. The outcome is that the churches are strengthened (v. 5).

When James Hudson Taylor went to serve as a missionary in China in the 19th century, he was unusual among Western missionaries in that he wore Chinese clothes. Working on the same basis as Paul, he did not want his Western-style clothes to be an obstacle to the gospel of Jesus being heard and welcomed by Chinese people. He also followed early Christian practice in translating the scriptures into several local languages, again to help Chinese people to hear and respond to the gospel message.

The challenge of crosscultural mission is great, and today it still requires the creativity and flexibility of Paul and Hudson Taylor. Their flexibility stemmed from their heartfelt service of Jesus Christ, placing people's need to hear and respond to him above any personal preference or desire. There's a challenge here for Christians today who enter others' cultural worlds so that the others might enter God's world of love and welcome.

6 Clarity of call—followed by problems

Acts 16:11–40

After being prevented by God from entering one place after another, Paul and his companions (now including Silas, not Barnabas: 15:39–40) have received clearance, through a vision, to go to the province of Macedonia (16:6–10). Problems await them in Philippi, a major city of Macedonia (v. 12), so confidence in God's call will be important in sustaining their ministry.

Problem 1 is the lack of a synagogue, Paul's usual starting point for evangelism. Paul has the imagination to seek a praying group by the river, and the courage to speak publicly with women (v. 13)—not something that many men would do in that world. God opens Lydia's heart to the gospel, and she welcomes Paul and his companions to her household (vv. 14–15).

Problem 2 is a demonised slave-girl who announces Paul's identity and mission (vv. 16–17). In the Gospels, other demonised people recognise dJesus' identity (for example, Luke 4:34–35), and Jesus' response was always to silence the demons. Paul is greatly disturbed and burdened by the girl's words ('annoyed' in the NRSV doesn't quite convey the sense) and, by God's power, the name of Jesus Christ, he frees her.

Problem 3 is caused by the slave-girl's deliverance, for public disorder follows and Paul and Silas are beaten and imprisoned (vv. 19–24). What must it have been like for them to sit in the innermost cell, reserved for the worst offenders (v. 24), knowing that God had called them to this place? And yet we find them singing praise to God (v. 25). They keep their eyes on God amid this third threat to the mission to which God has called them and, marvellously, God not only acts through the earthquake to release them (v. 26) but also brings the jailer and his family to faith in Jesus (vv. 27–34).

Problem 4 is that the city magistrates now want them out of the way as soon as possible (vv. 35–36). Paul confronts the authorities with their improper actions to ensure that the believing community he leaves behind in Philippi will be safe from official harrassment (vv. 37–39).

The clarity of God's call to a place or task can indicate that things will be tough there—and the clarity of call is what will sustain people called to tough places in Jesus' name today. Such situations need faith, imagination, and eyes fixed on the God who calls.

Guidelines

To share the gospel by word and deed with others, especially people from different cultural worlds, is a demanding but vital task for the church. Evangelism is not a merely human enterprise, however. It requires imagination combined with the work of God.

The mission to Jewish people needed imagination, for the Jews needed to understand how their Messiah could have been killed by the Romans after being handed over by their own leaders. There were several different expectations of a Messiah in Jesus' day, but none like that. The early believers dug deep into scripture to find stories, prophecies and psalms that explained how a suffering Messiah could be God's agent in redeeming the world. This message needed divinely inspired imagination, fed by the teaching that Jesus left his disciples; it also required the believers to allow God to burst the banks of their imagination and include 'even the Gentiles'.

In some churches, we feel safe in sharing the Christian faith with people like us; we know how to communicate with them and can rely on well-worn ways of doing so. The message of Acts is that God calls us not to stop there but to reach out to those who are *not* like us—the Lystran pagans (14:8–20) and the Antioch Gentiles (13:44–48).

Where is God calling your church to extend itself in this way? Might it be through a partnership with an ethnically different church? Might it be in serving a community in need, such as asylum seekers, people in poverty, single parents or people with mental health issues? Might it be in doing these things in the name of Jesus so that people learn of God's love for them in Jesus Christ? We must ask these questions to be faithful to the Acts vision of a church that exists to reach out, engage with others and share the gospel message with them. How could you encourage your church community to ask these questions?

FURTHER READING

Beverly R. Gaventa, *Acts* (Abingdon New Testament Commentary), Abingdon, 2003.
Tom Wright, *Acts for Everyone*, SPCK, 2008.

1 Timothy

Since the early 19th century, a large and influential body of scholarly opinion has rejected the view that Paul wrote this letter, arguing that historical, linguistic and stylistic factors point to the author's being a later admirer of Paul who impersonated him, possibly incorporating fragments of genuine Pauline material. However, this reconstruction poses as many questions as it purports to answer. For example, in focusing on the supposedly non-Pauline elements, it ignores those features that are unmistakably Pauline. The internal church difficulties reflected in the letter (anticipated in Acts 20:29–31) fit a date in the 60s, but the Ephesian church was marked by a well-documented orthodoxy at the close of the first century, when the pseudepigrapher is supposed to have written.

Accepting genuine Pauline authorship presupposes that the letter was written during a period subsequent to Acts 28, when Paul enjoyed a further time of freedom before his final arrest and imprisonment in Rome—and that is the position adopted in these notes.

Timothy had been associated with Paul since the second missionary journey (Acts 16:1–3) and was now in Ephesus. Paul had already written once, on his way to Macedonia, to instruct and encourage him in his pastoral oversight (see 1 Timothy 1:3). A feature of the letter is the note of urgency. Timothy is to 'command and teach these things' (4:11). So the theme of these notes is his urgent pastoral priorities.

Quotations are taken from the New International Version of the Bible.

1 The urgent priority of sound teaching

1 Timothy 1

In his introduction Paul uses the contemporary conventions of letter writing, as was his custom, but he suffuses them with Christian meaning. 'Mercy' is added to his normative 'grace and peace', possibly in view of the growing consciousness of God's mercy in his own life, evident in verses 13 and 16.

Timothy's top pastoral priority must be to guard the truth of the gospel and defend it from error. The danger here in Ephesus is apparently not from outsiders infiltrating the church but from leaders offering diseased teaching within the church, fulfilling the prophecy delivered by Paul in Acts 20:30.

Christian doctrine is not some cold, sterile, dead orthodoxy but a warm, vibrant, living faith, the dimensions of which are encapsulated in verse 5. It is not to be diluted by obscurantist disputes and controversies.

Paul upheld the value of the Old Testament law (v. 8), but the law was being misunderstood and misused by the false teachers (v. 7). In verses 9–10 Paul defines its purpose in terms of categories of law-breakers, six expressed in very general terms and eight more specific, but he returns in verse 11 to the central standard of truth, the gospel, by which everything is to be measured. The best way to learn to spot a forgery is to become totally familiar with the genuine article. Similarly, false teaching becomes obvious when we are fully conversant with the gospel.

Verses 12–17 continue to develop this focus. The gospel is a life-changing force. While Paul presents his own conversion as evidence of this, it is clear that the heart of the gospel is Christ Jesus and all that he has done in saving sinners—his grace, the outpouring of faith and love in him, his mercy and his patience. The heart of the gospel is faith in Jesus as Lord and his gift of eternal life.

Verse 17 concludes this section with a doxology ascribing honour and glory to God. Its origin is probably liturgical but its juxtaposition with the thanksgiving to Christ is suggestive of a high view of the person of Christ.

A characteristic of Paul's style is its expansiveness. References to God, Christ and Timothy are expanded with richly descriptive additions. The same can be said of his statements of gospel truths. It is noteworthy, therefore, that the reference to Hymenaeus and Alexander (v. 20) is so restrained. We might have expected a vituperative attack, but Paul's restraint is both salutary and instructive.

2 The urgent priority of prayer

It would be all too easy to dive into the closing section of this chapter and get embroiled in the kind of controversy and acrimony that chapter 1 is so vehemently against. The focus of the chapter is not primarily the roles of men and women but the importance of prayer, its purpose and prerequisites.

The first thing to notice is the scope of prayer, indicated by the repetition of the word 'all', which occurs (in the original) six times in the first six verses. It is worth meditating on these expressions of 'all', which challenge a prayer life that has become selfish, narrow or sterile.

Verse 1 reminds us that there is variety in prayer, which can include specific requests, a measure of formality, bold intercession and thankfulness. The different words used for prayer are not intended to be narrowly prescriptive but suggest variety in both format and occasion. Note, in verse 2, four aspects of the good lifestyle that pleases God and that cannot be attained without his enabling through prayer.

God has a comprehensive plan of salvation, which has been carried out through the mission and mediation of Christ Jesus, and an integral part of that plan, involving us, is prayer. Verses 3–6 reinforce the truth that prayer is not a matter of bending God to our will but of orienting ourselves towards his will and purpose.

Appropriate and authentic witness is an important factor in the New Testament message, and Paul presents his credentials in verse 7.

Verses 8–10 remind us that prayer can be effective only when integrated into a consistent Christian way of life, in both its positive and its negative aspects. There is not such a change of emphasis between verses 8 and 9 as some translations might suggest. The focus is still on prayer, and Paul's instructions for a lifestyle consistent with prayer are addressed to women as well as men, although much more is said to women (in verses 9–15) concerning modesty, decency, propriety, good deeds, education, quietness (not 'silence', but quietness in the sense that we find it in verse 2), submission, faith, love and holiness. The aims of verse 2 are again evident in verses 9–15.

It is important to read Paul's instructions in their original context of a letter to a specific church situation, the exact details of which we cannot know with certainty.

3 The urgent priority of church leadership

1 Timothy 3

This chapter begins with the second of the 'trustworthy sayings', and verses 2–7 emphasise the urgency of these instructions (brought out in the NIV's repeated 'must'). Throughout the Bible we discover that God's government is mediated through human leadership, which is both an immense privilege and a sobering responsibility.

It is hard to avoid seeing the traditional terms 'bishop' and 'deacon' through 21st-century-tinted glasses. They indicate oversight and service respectively. As 'overseers', the task of church leaders is not to do everything but to see that everything is done; and, as Jesus taught and demonstrated, the essence of leadership is service (see Mark 10:42–44).

Verses 1–7 outline the qualifications for the office of overseer, or bishop (*episkopos*), in 15 requirements, ten positive and five negative. It has been observed that these are neither distinctively nor exclusively Christian qualities. They encompass what we might call circles of contact: marriage, family, church, society and the enemy (the devil). The church is not a secret society but is salt and light in the world, with its leaders leading the way.

In verse 8, Paul introduces the qualifications of deacons with 'in the same way'. (The same Greek word is used in 2:9, where 'also' is a poor translation.) No hierarchical structure is in view here. Nine qualifications are given for *diakonoi* (the regular word for servants), six positive and three negative. Note the phrase 'in the same way' again in verse 11, with reference to the *gunaikes*, which can mean either 'women' or 'wives', according to context—hence, women deacons or wives of deacons. Four qualities are outlined for them, three positive and one negative. Verse 13 points to the reward for good service: personal assurance, recognition in the community and confident standing in Christ Jesus.

Although the focus of this chapter has tended towards general integrity, Paul returns in verses 15–16 to the specific distinctives of Christian belief and behaviour—the purpose of the church and the centrality of the person and work of Christ. This is expressed in hymnic form, composed around a series of contrasts, including flesh and spirit, angels and humans, earth and heaven, in which the message of the New Testament is encapsulated in six short lines.

4 The urgent priority of watchfulness

1 Timothy 4

Paul returns once more to the strategic importance of sound teaching and the danger of false teaching. Verse 1 brings the first mention of the (Holy) Spirit in this letter, a Spirit who is instrumental not only in the initial role of inspiration but also in illumination and application.

Verse 1 gives us insight into the spiritual forces behind false teaching, while verse 2 describes the human messengers who carry it. Verse 3a gives specific examples of their teaching, followed by general principles for testing them, with particular reference to the veto on eating certain foods. Verses 4 and 5 enunciate a general principle stemming from our belief in God as creator.

From verse 6, Paul addresses Timothy very directly. The word often translated 'minister' in this verse is *diakonos*, used in the previous chapter for 'deacon', reminding us that ministry is essentially service. Throughout this letter we find references to 'faith' (that is, believing), and 'the faith', meaning the body of truth on which faith is based. It is this that enables good service to others, nourishes the servant and underpins good teaching to follow. Everything about it is 'good', unlike the godless myths and old wives' tales being peddled by some.

In verses 7b and 8, Paul introduces the concept of training in godliness. It is worth exploring the parallels with physical training (which is not without value but cannot compare with the greater value of godliness). Grammatically, the 'trustworthy saying' of verse 9 may refer either back to verse 8 or forward to verse 10.

Verses 11–16 continue the strong focus on the need for teaching. Note how many times teaching is mentioned in this chapter. It must be done with authority. It must be accompanied by example. It must be based on Scripture. It must be worked on diligently. There should be evidence of progress, which will call for perseverance.

The construction 'both... and' which appears at the end of verse 16 opens up a number of lessons in this chapter. Paul's concerns are about both the Spirit and good human teachers; both demons and bad human teachers; both the word of God and prayer; both physical training and training in godliness; both the present and the future; both teaching and example; both the gift and wholehearted diligence; both the word of prophecy and the laying on of hands; both life and doctrine; both yourself and your hearers.

5 The urgent priority of pastoral care

1 Timothy 5

The biggest difference between Israel and the church is that Israel is a nation whereas the church is a family. It is family relationships that should dictate the approach of the young pastor Timothy in his dealings with his fellow church members of both sexes, both his contemporaries and those older than him. We should never undervalue the amazing fact that, by grace, God has brought us into his family.

A comparison of verses 1–16 with a parallel passage, Titus 2, reveals where a major problem in Ephesus lay. God's concern for the care of widows is evident throughout the Old Testament (for example, Exodus 22:22–24; Psalm 68:5; Isaiah 1:17, 23) and it remained of importance in New Testament times (see Acts 6:1). Here in 1 Timothy 5, the amount of space it occupies is significant.

We create a false dichotomy if we drive a wedge between evangelism and social care: the church has a duty to engage in both. Of course, in New Testament times, there was no welfare state and Christian believers could be disowned by both pagan and Jewish families.

It is not easy to understand fully the situation that Timothy had to address but the following principles are clear. There is a duty of care towards widows within the natural family (vv. 3–8, 16), there is a duty of appropriate behaviour on the part of the widow who is 'really in need' (vv. 3, 5, 9–10), and there is a duty of care within the church generally in cases where a widow has no other means of support (vv. 3, 9). It is worth noting that those in greatest need still have a valuable contribution to make.

Any welfare programme suffers from the problem that some needy people will not apply for help, while others, less in need, will try to take unfair advantage of the provision. The Bible is realistic enough to recognise a similar problem in the early church, as verses 11–15 suggest, and it is equally realistic in its approach to the undeserving.

The final part of this chapter, from verse 17 onward, returns to the role, rewards and rights of those who lead as elders. Timothy receives a solemn charge to avoid partiality and favouritism and to develop patience and purity, along with some very practical health advice.

6 Final instructions

1 Timothy 6

The first two verses remind us that slaves were a normal part of the first-century household and, understandably, needed instruction concerning their new 'freedom in Christ', whether they belonged to Christian or non-Christian masters. Slaves could take encouragement from the fact that even the praiseworthy elders were 'under the yoke' (see 5:17–18). God's name and teaching, respect and top-quality service are priorities that we can all take into the modern workplace.

The motives of the false teachers hinted at in 3:3 ('… not a lover of money') are now addressed more fully in verses 3–10 and 17–19. It is clear that their 'unhealthy interest' in controversy, along with its baneful results (vv. 4–5), is motivated by the desire for financial gain. False teaching is seldom motivated by intellectual issues alone.

Verse 6 is one of those 'stand alone' verses that should be imprinted on the hearts of every Christian in well-off Western society. 'Contentment' is a Stoic-Cynic virtue. Here, however, it means not self-sufficiency but sufficiency in Christ, as in Philippians 4:10–13. Verses 7–8 echo both Job 1:21 and the teaching of Jesus in Matthew 6:25–34.

In verses 9–10, the negative results of a desire to get rich are contrasted with that positive value of godliness with contentment. Verse 10 contains one of the most misquoted statements in the Bible: take careful note of what it actually says!

Verses 11–12 contain four imperatives addressed to Timothy, introduced by the emphatic 'But you, man of God…'. They concern flight and pursuit, fight and capture. They are followed by a solemn charge calling to mind Timothy's 'good confession' before many witnesses and before God, looking back to the example of Christ and looking forward to his return, climaxing in a richly descriptive doxology.

Although verse 16 looks like the end of the letter, verse 17 returns to the subject of riches, both their dangers and their opportunities. Yet again, Timothy is instructed to 'command' those who are rich in this present world, with seven imperatives, two negative and five positive. The rich people's motivation should be the uncertainty of wealth, the generosity of God and preparation for the coming age. They, like Timothy (v. 12), must 'take hold' of the life that is truly life.

In his final words, Paul once more addresses Timothy himself: in the light of the dangers around him, he must guard what is true and turn away from what is false.

Guidelines

For meditation and further reflection:

- Imagine yourself writing a letter to your own local church. What would you identify as the urgent priorities in it and how far do they match the priorities emphasised by Paul?
- How does Paul's letter help us to deal with contemporary issues of age and youth, male and female roles, and church government?
- If you had to choose six favourite verses from 1 Timothy, what would they be and why?

FURTHER READING

John Stott, *The Message of 1 Timothy and Titus* (The Bible Speaks Today), IVP, 1996 (entry level).

Gordon D. Fee, *1 and 2 Timothy, Titus* (New International Biblical Commentary), Hendrickson, 1995 (mid-range).

George W. Knight, *The Pastoral Epistles: A commentary on the Greek text* (New International Greek Testament Commentary), Eerdmans/Paternoster, 1992 (advanced).

Daniel

The book of Daniel is usually introduced with a focus on its historical settings and/or its complex literary development—in other words, the scaffolding of the book rather than its point. Ironically, the reputation of the first six chapters as 'children's stories' probably does more justice to the issues at stake in the text. Quite rightly, children read about the fiery furnace and the lions' den as narratives of God in conflict with the enemy, delivering the faithful from trial and tribulation. Israel almost certainly passed these stories down through its traditions just because they gave images of faithful life under conditions of extreme difficulty, where life might be understood as being lived 'in the furnace' or 'among lions'. If not quite allegories, they nevertheless contain a strong metaphorical component, seeking to redescribe the reader's world in the vivid terms of the tale being told.

Thus, the stories relate to the sixth century BC in Babylon, home of Daniel himself, the hero of most of these chapters. They relate to the second century BC, when Israel wondered again if God would be faithful in the face of the horrors of the Seleucid onslaught. They relate to the time of Jesus, with God taking a stand against evil, and they relate to our own times, if we have eyes to see it.

When and how the book was written turns out to make almost no difference to any of these points, so we shall pass over such matters in silence and read the stories instead.

In chapter 7, the book takes a sudden turn. The genre becomes 'apocalyptic', a word derived from the Greek word for 'revelation'. Apocalyptic literature has a reputation for being about the end of the world. Better to say that it is about the end of the world *as we know it*: it is about reorientating the way we think of the world in which we live.

Key characteristics of apocalyptic include fantastical imagery (particularly beasts, interestingly signposted in chapter 6) and a general sense of darkness in mood and expectation. In Daniel's case, the subject matter turns decisively to visions and their interpretations. The confident dream-interpreter of chapters 2 and 4 is suddenly at a loss and needs angelic help.

Readers of the book will know how he feels—these are difficult chapters to interpret—but we will focus on key themes and try to hold on to the hope at the heart of it. Wise reading, more than historical expertise, will remain key.

Quotations are taken from the New Revised Standard Version unless otherwise indicated.

1 Alien territory

Daniel 1

Two short verses at the beginning tell us everything we need to know about the disorientated context for the rest of the book. Jerusalem has fallen, because the Lord let it happen (v. 2). The temple has been ransacked and we have been taken to Babylon, 'the land of Shinar'.

So, then, we can imagine Daniel, dazed and confused, awaking to this strange new world in verse 3 and struggling to keep up with developments. This has two interesting effects upon readers of the book. First, we too struggle to keep up. These are narratives of an alien world in a distant time, set amid court intrigue in what seems to be an ancient Babylonian school of witchcraft and wizardry. Even our normal biblical reference points are gone: there will be no mention for some time yet of the name of the Lord ('Yhwh' being conspicuous by its absence).

Second, we are invited to see our own world as strange. We live and move in a world overly familiar with governmental intrigue and the machinations of power, a world deeply engaged in education and arguments over how to handle it, and even a world with competing concerns over diet and the ethics of food. In one sense, then, the book of Daniel feels strangely contemporary, but in another sense, we realise as we read it that we do not know our way around such a world from God's point of view. What will count as faithfulness in this alien environment? This is a key question both for our reading and for our lives today.

Daniel 1 foregrounds at least three issues for reflection: the requirement that Daniel study the Babylonian dark arts, the imposition of foreign names on our four protagonists (v. 7), and concerns over the royal diet, a diet that they reject. It is the third issue, the diet, on which they take a stand, at considerable risk. Despite various theories, the text does not really tell us why this one matters so much. Perhaps it is a line in the sand.

Is it possible to take an ethical or theological stand in the city at the heart of empire? Just because we cannot fight all the battles at once, does that mean that no battle is worth fighting? Daniel 1 seems to be a story of low-key resistance in anticipation of bigger conflicts to come.

2 Dangerous dreams

Daniel 2:1–24

Hebrew-speaking readers of Daniel would have had their disorientation ramped up considerably at the start of chapter 2. Not only does King Nebuchadnezzar appear to be calling for an interpretation of a dream he will not relate, but the whole story lurches into Aramaic in verse 4. Aramaic was the international trade language of the region, of which Hebrew was effectively the local dialect. Readers were therefore being required to engage in this account through the stilted tones of an unfamiliar formal language. The effect would have been like attending a social event several levels more formal than was comfortable—not knowing their way around, what to do or say, or what reactions were expected.

There is a lot of outrage, indignation and exaggeration in these accounts. King Nebuchadnezzar, in particular, is depicted as over the top. What sort of madman won't even describe his dream, if he wants it interpreted? Some commentators suggest that he doesn't really know it himself. All he knows is that he has awoken troubled and is angry with his whole ineffective retinue. There is a kind of incipient insanity about the king, which will only get worse.

Daniel is calm, by contrast. He models the body politic—astute in matters of power and polite in ways that defuse the situation—even though the real turning point occurs in his own dream, his strange 'vision of the night' (v. 19). Daniel sings a song of praise in response to the God who 'knows what is in the darkness, and light dwells with him' (v. 22).

To paraphrase, then: Nebuchadnezzar is afraid of the dark, whereas Daniel waits upon a light that will overcome the darkness. Neither the king nor the prophet, nor the author of the book itself, is in a hurry to tell us the dream yet. The focus is on the one who reveals, in his own good time—as yet unnamed, but the power *above* the throne, as it were.

3 The empire struck down

Daniel 2:25–49

We come to the dream itself. Today's passage starts with a reference to Daniel being brought before the king, arguably for the first time if we compare the 'second year' of Nebuchadnezzar's reign (2:1) with the 'end' of 'three years' (1:5, 18) during which Daniel was being trained.

It's a dream of a multi-part statue, collapsed by the impact of a stone cut out 'not by human hands' (v. 34), and described in Daniel's interpretation as a succession of empires that shall rise and fall until there comes an indestructible kingdom set up by the God of heaven (v. 44).

There is a real temptation for readers to head off immediately down the path of decoding the dream, trying to work out which empire was which and how each one relates to the different materials (gold, iron, and so on); we could debate whether the reference to the feet made partly of iron and partly of clay might denote some kind of composite kingdom, such as the Medo-Persian empire, or another political entity created by marriage alliances (see v. 43). It is worth noting, though, that the chapter itself gives very few clues about how to do the decoding.

Instead, we note the decline from 'gold' to less impressive substances: Nebuchadnezzar is condemned to losing his empire at the same time as being informed that his is the most majestic of all. We can note the lack of interest in the text in how the dream (one statue, toppled all at once by one stone) matches the interpretation (a series of empires, finally replaced by one 'rock'), and we might suspect that Nebuchadnezzar really does have no idea what is going on. He worships Daniel, who, ever the politician, overlooks the theological impropriety and uses the occasion to get his friends installed in high places (v. 49). Who is really playing whom here?

As to whether the stone that causes the statue to stumble is Christ: well, yes it is, if we have eyes to see it, but then it can also be many other divine interventions in world affairs. Empires look as solid as statues, but they never last. Even when it is the king who concludes, 'Your God is God of gods' (v. 47), that king's days are numbered.

4 Life in the furnace

Another story; another statue; another tale of King Nebuchadnezzar urging the impossible, looking ridiculous, and ending up extravagantly affirming the praise of the God of Daniel and his friends. Another picture of life in the midst of empire?

One clue to a powerful traditional reading of Daniel 3 is in Deuteronomy 4:20: 'The Lord has taken you and brought you out of the iron-smelter, out of Egypt' (several translations say 'iron furnace' here). Another clue is in the great prophet of return from exile, found in Isaiah 40—55: 'I have tested you in the furnace of adversity' (48:10), or 'When you walk through fire you shall not be burned, and the flame shall not consume you' (43:2). Daniel 3 is, in many ways, a narrative depicting the same ideas.

The people of God in this chapter are represented by the more-or-less composite figure of Shadrach, Meshach and Abednego. They will not appear in the book again, and we never see them acting individually. They are God's people, and the trigger for the furnace episode is that they ignore Nebuchadnezzar's bizarre decree that all should worship an enormous statue at the sound of his travelling jazz band.

It is not irrelevant to this story that it includes multiple semi-comic repetitions of long lists of self-important description. The narrative is making fun of the pomposity of empire. As well as repetition, there is exaggeration—a furnace heated seven times hotter than it needs to be, for instance.

The core moment of truth, however, is intense and awful: it is a declaration of unswerving faithfulness from the friends in verses 17–18, recognising that all may not turn out well but refusing to compromise. The result is swift: they experience the deadly fire.

At its heart, the resolution involves a mysterious divine/angelic presence coming to be with the people of God in the furnace of adversity. We may want to say, and to pray, that God will deliver us from adversity. But the first thing Israel says, in this story as elsewhere, is that God comes to join God's people in the midst of adversity. That's a word of life for the darkest of days, and the book of Daniel anticipates that there will be many of those.

5 Method in the madness

This chapter offers a final version of the narrative of Nebuchadnezzar's hubris, subsequent humbling, and final honouring of God. It is presented as a letter from the king describing a terrifying dream (vv. 1–18), followed by Daniel's interpretation of it (vv. 19–27), and ending with a narrative of the resulting events.

Is it important to note that Daniel, by this point, seems to have grown fond of the king, wishing that the disastrous implications of the dream would apply to someone other than Nebuchadnezzar (v. 19)? The tone of this chapter will be worth comparing with the confrontation to come in chapter 5.

Nevertheless, Daniel's counsel is without compromise: 'Atone for your sins with righteousness, and your iniquities with mercy to the oppressed' (v. 27). The text here is not straightforward, and many (Protestant) translations swerve to avoid the implication that sins can be paid for through acts of righteousness and mercy. It makes sense, though, that the king whose decisions will impact God's people in such precarious circumstances should be enjoined to act rightly and love mercy, in order to make things right with God. This is how a king is supposed to act, after all.

There is an oddity to the final part of the story. Nebuchadnezzar gets rather full of himself (v. 30) and, as a result, becomes like a wild animal, going mad in some ill-defined way. But when he is restored, after realising that he is to bless the Most High God rather than himself, his final words still do not sound like the words of a humble man (v. 36).

Maybe this is the best we can hope for in engaging with a king who, although, deep down, is rather over-impressed with his own capabilities, will at least listen to reason, or even to truth as delivered through a prophet. Is the book of Daniel, in certain key ways, realistic about our prospects for engaging with the government?

6 The writing on the wall

Daniel 5

From this story comes the celebrated statement, 'the writing is on the wall', meaning that the end is at hand and nothing can be done about it.

The switch to King Belshazzar in the narrative appears to have the function of moving on to consider a king who, in contrast to Nebuchadnezzar, will not listen to reason. Daniel's tone in addressing this king (v. 17) is strikingly dismissive. There is no sense that he wants to do deals with Belshazzar, or wishes that it might be the king's enemies who suffer the fate described. Note, too, that when we reach chapters 7—8, with their own terrifying visions of the night, these troubles are also ascribed to the years of Belshazzar's reign. The point is this: not every king is Nebuchadnezzar. Know your imperial enemy; discern the difference between the time to negotiate and the time to confront. Be as wise as a seer and as innocent as a Daniel.

Chapter 5 describes, more or less, an orgy in the palace, with the party-goers drinking from vessels stolen from the Jerusalem temple. It is a blunt abuse of what counted as holy in Israel. When God intervenes with a vision of a hand writing on a wall, the result is chaos. We read in verse 6 that Belshazzar's 'limbs gave way'. Scholars of the odd language of this verse suggest that it was not just that his legs gave way, causing him to sit with a bump, but that some of his internal organ control was lost in the moment, too. The scene in chapter 5 is describing a dishonourable mess.

Daniel's eventual intervention does two things. First, it rehearses the lessons that should have been learned from Nebuchadnezzar and charges Belshazzar with ignoring them. Second, it interprets the strange Aramaic inscription from the hand of God. By dint of the traditional language of English translations, we can paraphrase the inscription in the words of media guru Marshall McLuhan: 'the medium is the message'. What God says to Belshazzar is, in effect, 'The writing is on the wall.'

Guidelines

The stories in Daniel 1—5 offer much food for thought with respect to how we discern the voice of God in the midst of our cultural contexts, and how we engage with the people in power around us.

Daniel and Joseph are the two characters in the Bible who operated particularly by way of dream interpretation. Both were located in foreign territory and both seem to have had gifts that related to their contexts. What could we conclude about the gifts God might give us in our own contexts? How do people organise their lives and recognise guidance today? We will think, perhaps, of celebrity culture or the world of online 'experts': would Daniel and his friends today be willing to battle through reality TV shows, or serve as interns for news services and face the consequences of the struggle to be faithful in such 'alien' environments?

A second consideration is God's sovereignty. This image, often misunderstood, relates to God as the one within whose kingdom events take place. Much of the book of Daniel plays out narratives about who is really in power. We should note that power does not easily equate to control or to direct intervention in events. Which situations currently trouble us most in terms of who has power over them? How helpful is it that the book of Daniel itself lacks resolution over some of these issues?

Finally, do we underestimate, in our spiritual lives, the power of a good story? Is it worth considering reading a Christian biography or history as a testimony to the God of Daniel? Some of the most profound lessons we learn come clothed in the specifics of people's stories. Look out for stories that might illuminate the ways of God in our own 'empire' today.

1 A night of beasts

Daniel 6

The new king, Darius, is markedly more sympathetic to Daniel, but still, as this story makes clear, more than able to trouble Israel. He is described as 'Darius the Mede', a celebrated case of an identification that has confounded historians over the years, although it makes very little difference to the way we read the story. What matters is that Darius is presented as a good king and fundamentally sympathetic to Daniel, thus rounding out the book's trio of rulers of various kinds.

The story is well known—a Sunday school classic. A group of schemers require prayer to be made only to the king; Daniel prays to God in deliberate defiance (knowing 'that the document had been signed', v. 10), ends up being thrown into a den of lions, as promised, and is kept safe through the night by an angel.

The significance of the story can be missed through our overfamiliarity. Again, the narrative uses a metaphor for life in exile to describe the experiences of the people of God. The image here is of a faithful man surrounded by beasts. Readers of the book are presumably supposed to remember this picture in the next chapter, when Daniel's famous vision portrays the nations around Israel as beasts. In other words, the book itself is pointing towards the analogy between 'Daniel among the lions' and 'Israel among the nations'.

It is also a story that refuses to accept the empire's self-presentation: the celebrated status of the law of the Medes and Persians as 'unchangeable' (repeated in verses 8, 12 and 15) is overturned by Darius in verse 26 without a second-thought. Persevere for long enough and the most insurmountable barriers may be overcome.

We can almost read this story today imagining it as the tale of Daniel, the distinguished politician, being caught out by the Persian government's equivalent of the tabloid press. He chooses simply to continue his life of prayer and leave the consequences to God. Another later context also comes to mind. After Daniel has been consigned to death, in the morning the stone is rolled away and he is discovered to be alive. Does that ring any bells? Easter bells?

2 A night-vision of beasts

Daniel 7:1–15

We come now to the key chapter of the book. The last verse of our reading (v. 15) highlights the sense of spiritual darkness and fear that comes into the book at this point.

Daniel recounts a dream. Again we must be careful about the temptation to focus on decoding, but the sequence of images is clear. There are four beasts coming out of the chaos of the sea. They are, in turn, a lion-eagle-human figure (thus capable of representing a range of views of one power/empire?); a bear (not so positive?); a four-headed winged leopard (no, really!); and then, as if these had not been bad enough, some kind of monster. To us, with our knowledge of the dream in chapter 2, these beasts look like a succession of four empires, gradually increasing in their terror and/or threat to Israel.

The fourth beast has ten horns (v. 7), which we should probably read as a (lengthy) series of kings. The additional horn (v. 8) is described as both 'little' and as causing considerable trouble, thereby perhaps both 'belittling' him and recognising the danger he represents.

The second half of the chapter will begin to tease out the details, but, before Daniel can worry about that, he sees a courtroom scene in heaven. God, as the Ancient One, makes a very impressive judge (in language later borrowed for the book of Revelation) and summarily destroys the trouble-making final beast and its problematic tenth horn. It turns out that real power belongs not to any of these beasts but to 'one like a son of man' (the NRSV's gender-neutral 'human being'), arriving to be presented before God (v. 13).

In other words, in true apocalyptic style, all is not as it seems in our world. God really is in control, and the 'son of man' figure plays some key role in enacting his judgement. Christian readings of this chapter inevitably and rightly see this figure as Jesus, with language that points to a dramatic 'coming' before God. While Daniel himself is not thinking about 'the second coming' (he has more immediate concerns with the beast-like fourth empire), the image will, in due course, serve powerfully to bring Christians hope in the face of persecution.

3 Interpreting the vision

Daniel 7:16–28

Daniel turns to a handily-placed 'dreams and visions' tour guide for some help with what he has just seen. It may be helpful for us to realise that they go over the details several times here.

The first run-through (vv. 17–18) is so brief that it leaves out almost all the detail. (It is also, incidentally, somewhat puzzling, in effectively describing each 'empire' as a 'king', although we can see the point.) So Daniel has to probe with a more specific question. Verses 19–22 recap the middle section of the dream, concerning the fourth beast and the final horn—their arrogance, the resulting conflict and their judgement. The next five verses

(vv. 23–27) therefore focus on that section, elaborating on the disaster of the fourth beast/final horn, on God's judgement and victory and (perhaps key) on the giving of dominion finally to 'the people of the holy ones of the Most High'. This description may refer to humans and angels together as God's 'holy army'.

All of this imagery can work in generic terms. Evil empires rise and fall, but even the most evil among them will ultimately suffer judgement. If the message is the same as the one we heard in Daniel 1—6, the tenor and urgency of it have darkened considerably. That's part of the problem with a 'decoding' approach: it aims to explain which empires and kings are in view, but can, in the process, lose the terrifying nature of the imagery (see v. 28).

However, the vision can also work in more historically specific terms, too. Scholars of Israel's history, partly working with the scheme of Daniel 11 in view (which also lists various empires, kings, and enemies of Israel), think that the horns represent a succession of rulers during the third and second centuries BC, ending with the vicious 'little horn' himself, Antiochus IV Epiphanes, the Seleucid king who reigned from 175 to 164BC. This makes the book of Daniel a powerful word of hope in the face of apparently unstoppable oppression during the time of the Jewish revolt in the 160s BC. (The details can be read in the Apochryphal book of 1 Maccabees 1—4.)

Of course, in the end, it works both ways. A word of hope in the dark days of 164BC is a word of hope to all God's people oppressed anywhere, at any time. Is it also a description of the end of the world? Probably not so much.

4 Reading scripture; discerning the times

Daniel 9

Daniel 8—12 works over much of the same ground as Daniel 7 but in more detail. It also returns to the use of the Hebrew language (the language of insiders?). Perhaps the book represents several runs at trying to see God's hand in political events. We shall focus instead on some aspects of the way Daniel engages with this spiritual reality that is being unveiled to him.

Daniel 9:2–3 looks like a prototype of the personal 'quiet time'—prayer and Bible study in quiet reflection. In fact, it is striking to realise how seldom we see this practice in scripture. It is very rare in the Old Testament, not least because many individuals could not read—and, of course, in most cases, the scriptures themselves were still in the process of being written down. Daniel is probably reading Jeremiah 25 or 29, perhaps especially 29:10. The question is, then, when will the exile be over? The question drives Daniel to prayer.

There is much to learn from the way the prophet discerns the word of God for his own time from his reading of scripture. The text only says that he 'perceives' these things in scripture (v. 2) but the presentation of the whole book has emphasised that Daniel is a wise man, set apart for his commitment, obedience and willingness to persevere through trials. There is a lesson here about how a person of holy character is able to discern the word of God. The fact that he responds in prayer, with confession and intercession, also indicates the condition of heart and mind required to see what God wants to say in scripture. It is a salutary reminder in the midst of these forbidding chapters of ancient political and theological imagery.

All that can be said about the 'seventy weeks' discussion that ends the chapter is that the angel Gabriel is engaged in negotiating exactly what counts as exile and when it will end. The answer to the latter question is, to paraphrase Paul, 'when the fullness of time has come' (Galatians 4:4). So there is hope here, but not a lot, if we reflect on the overall tone of the discussion.

5 Spiritual warfare

Daniel 10

This chapter follows on from the emphasis in Daniel 9 on prayer. It also continues the theme of interaction with named angels, which is not common in scripture.

Three orientations may be helpful. Firstly, the word received by Daniel in verse 1 is not really explored here: it seems to be a kind of prophetic dress-rehearsal for the much longer vision recounted in chapter 11. Arguably, that vision is, in fact, the one mentioned in 10:1, about 'a great conflict', although 11:1 seems to give a separate, later date. The vision that Daniel sees in 10:5–8, however, is a different one and involves his interaction with an angelic figure who explains how Daniel's prayers are (or are not) working.

Secondly, this angelic figure tells Daniel some strange things. In effect, Daniel's prayers are important to the heavenly host and have been held in a queue for 21 days, while Michael has been sorting out some problems with the 'prince of Persia'. 'Prince' here seems to designate an angel in command. There are two named angels in the book—Gabriel (8:16; 9:21), who appears as 'the angel of the Lord' in Luke 1, and Michael (10:13, 21; 12:1), who is described as 'your chief prince', where the plural 'your' refers to the nation of Israel. Michael also appears as a kind of military angel in Jude 9 and Revelation 12:7. Most readers of the Bible are probably unaware of how restrained all this material is, in comparison with other Jewish texts of the time (1 Enoch is a good example), where long lists of hierarchies of angels are imagined organising the world. Daniel acknowledges this world-view but does not seem to get too excited about it.

Thirdly, and fundamentally, to pray is to engage in spiritual conflict. Also not obviously apparent to readers of Daniel is how little emphasis is placed in chapters 8—12 on armed uprising as the solution to Israel's problems. The focus—again, unlike in other texts—is not on political insurrection. It is on prayer. Some commentators even see Daniel 10 as a model of 'pacifist aggression'. God will do the 'fighting': our role is to pray.

6 Final hope

Daniel 12

Chapter 11 offers a lengthy account of Israel's history under various aggressors through the fifth to second centuries BC. This is little-known territory for most Bible readers, and can appear as rather more exotic than it was probably intended to be. It concludes with a discussion of 'the time of the end' (11:40). Without going into detail, it is best to see the final verses of chapter 11 as talking about the end of the struggle with Antiochus Epiphanes in 164BC, rather than the end of the world as we would understand it. It is not that this account describes what happened to Antiochus (he actually died of consumption in Persia in 164, whereas the text here imagines various elaborate military scenarios). Rather, the whole chapter focuses on the hope that his tyranny shall pass.

That hope is then underlined in 12:1–3, where it opens out into resurrection hope. Unusually for the Old Testament, we have here a powerful expectation of individual resurrection from the dead, buildings on ideas such as the national resurrection of Israel in Ezekiel's 'valley of dry bones' vision (Ezekiel 37). Death—even cruel death in the bitter fighting of the Jewish revolt—is not the end. In this context, verse 2 makes it clear that we must be faithful throughout this life, since the results of unfaithfulness will play out in the next.

Even so, we have to say that the book ends inconclusively. Daniel himself is not invited to understand all that he has seen (v. 9), and the end of Israel's suffering cannot be dated clearly (vv. 12–13). The repeated phrase 'a time, times and half a time' (7:25; 12:7, NIV) perhaps indicates a sudden intervention in the expected progression of things, and Daniel eagerly anticipates that intervention but does not live to see it. Instead, he 'rests' in anticipation (v. 13). Rather like Daniel, his readers look for the resurrection of the dead, and the life of the world to come.

Guidelines

From the moment when Darius allows Daniel to be thrown into the lions' den, the book is overwhelmed with beast imagery, as it describes the terrors of Israel's fragile position at the mercy of empire. Of course, the empires show no mercy at all, so it all comes down to God's mercy against human powers.

Is it significant that one of the Old Testament's most powerful images of God's victory in human affairs is crafted in the midst of such struggle? Forced to reflect on what really matters, Daniel sees the 'son of man' figure snatch a stunning victory out of the (monstrous) jaws of defeat. It's not so much that every cloud has a silver lining, rather, the light that overcomes the darkness is more visible in the darkest times. Those who pray for persecuted Christians around the world are reminded of this truth again and again. The book of Daniel really does suggest that such prayers are invested in the conflicts of spiritual forces—and that is surely why it is hard to remain faithful in such prayer. Let Daniel encourage you to keep going.

If apocalyptic imagery mirrors the realities of difficult situations, though, does it also reflect some of its disturbing light back on those parts of the world where we seem to live in peace and prosperity? Is the unveiling of the Babylonian, Persian, Greek and, in due course, Roman empires as 'beasts' a reminder that all is not as it seems? That is the great apocalyptic insight. Ask God for the gift of eyes to see and ears to hear the spiritual reality of the world around you.

In Daniel 9 we saw a wise man who was able to discern God's word for his own day. Throughout the book, in the midst of everything, wisdom reigns supreme. To conclude with a proverb: though it cost all you have, get wisdom! (see Proverbs 4:7, NIV).

FURTHER READING

John E. Goldingay, *Daniel* (Word Biblical Commentary), Word, 1987.

Daniel L. Smith-Christopher, 'Daniel' in L.E. Keck (ed.), *The New Interpreter's Bible* Volume 7, Abingdon Press, 1996.

Aaron B. Hebbard, *Reading Daniel as a Text in Theological Hermeneutics*, Pickwick, 2009.

Danna Nolan Fewell, *Circle of Sovereignty: Plotting politics in the book of Daniel*, Abingdon Press, 1991.

Philippians

For the purposes of these readings, I have followed the traditional hypothesis that the letter to the Philippians was written by Paul, sometime during his imprisonment at Rome (not Caesarea or Ephesus), between AD60 and 62. The recipients of the letter in Philippi had been introduced to the Christian message during the visit of Paul, Silas, Timothy and Luke, as recorded in Acts 16, around AD49. This was the first Christian church (founded by Paul, at least) in Europe.

Philippi had been built on a previous settlement and was named after Philip of Macedon (the father of Alexander the Great). It became a Roman military colony around 168BC, thus enduing its citizens, many of whom were retired soldiers, with the benefits of Roman citizenship. As Philippi was an outpost of Rome, the idea of dual citizenship would have been familiar to its inhabitants, as would the regal titles of 'lord' or 'saviour' bestowed on the emperor. Paul's letter is filled with references to the true Lord, the humble Saviour. The church as a colony of heaven is portrayed as anticipating the arrival of the true Emperor, the Lord Jesus. Thus, as citizens of heaven, the believers are encouraged to live in a manner worthy of their position.

These notes will seek to show how recent studies have identified that Paul adapted literary conventions of his day, expanding and developing the customary devices of a 'letter of friendship' to his own purposes. Those characteristics have been italicised to enable you to identify them easily. Recurrent themes within the letter have been noted in cross references within the notes.

As we ponder the text each day, we might also bear in mind that 'theology for Paul is not philosophical or academic in nature but is confessional and doxological' (Gordon Fee, *Paul's Letter to the Philippians*, Eerdmans, 1995, p. 47).

Quotations are taken from the English Standard Version of the Bible.

1 Joy in the church

Philippians 1:1–2

Although these two verses might be dismissed as mere courtesies, following the conventions of letter writing in the Greco-Roman world, they lead us to ponder anew the glorious mystery of what we rather cursorily designate 'the church'.

Paul, at the opening of his letter, follows the literary conventions of his age (naming both the author and the recipients, along with a salutation), but he also radically transforms the commonplace into a glorious declaration of the grace of God and an anticipation of the final completed abundant peace (*shalom*) of God. The local and the heavenly character of the Church in all ages is expressed. While dwelling locally within the Roman colony of Philippi, in Christ the believers are, in fact, 'saints'—that is, 'God's holy people'. Far from being isolated expressions of grace, in Christ the Philippian Christians have now become part of God's chosen covenant people (1 Peter 2:9–10). Before the ten commandments were given (Exodus 20) and ratified by the people (Exodus 24:6–8), God declared through Moses that the stateless nation of rescued captive slaves were a 'treasured possession among the peoples', becoming by divine grace 'a kingdom of priests, a holy nation' (Exodus 19:1–6).

Yet this mysterious body, the heavenly Church universal (whose citizenship is in heaven: Philippians 3:20), is mediated to the world through the visible local church. Although Paul mentions himself and Timothy as 'servants of Christ Jesus' by name, it is, in fact, the unnamed 'saints', overseers and deacons who comprise the local expression at Philippi. All are tokens and expressions of grace.

The same grace has transformed Paul's and Timothy's lives (1 Timothy 1:12–17; 2 Timothy 1:3–7). It was grace that enabled the wealthy businesswoman, Lydia, to hear God's word (Acts 16:14–15). Grace transformed the lives of a young woman bound by the spirit of divination and a hardened Philippian jailer (Acts 16:16–17, 33–34), enabling them to become partners in the gospel (Philippians 1:5; 4:14). Divine grace and singing in a prison; miraculous intervention through earthquakes and persecution; a colony of heaven in the midst of human culture and history—such is the experience of the Church universal, manifested locally.

2 Joy in thanksgiving

Philippians 1:3–11

In popular culture, negative portrayals of the church abound. Media reports of sexual, financial or other misconduct within the church, in addition to hurtful experiences of individuals whom we know, might lead us to be tempted to abandon 'church' and to go it alone.

The New Testament itself records the weaknesses of the newly formed churches and the many frustrations experienced by the apostle Paul. When considered aright, however, the mystery and glory of the universal Church and the imperfectly reflected mystery and glory of the local church will dissuade the lone ranger Christian from embarking on an isolated pilgrimage.

In our passage today, Paul, following the letter-writing conventions of his day by *addressing and greeting the recipients*, directs his readers' thoughts to the life-source of the universal Church, namely God himself (v. 3). This recognition of the work of God, in individual lives and in the church locally, stimulates in Paul a profound thankfulness to God 'in all my remembrance of you'.

The recognition of God's sovereign activity creates a joyful confidence that the creator of these renewed lives in Christ has a plan to bring the work to fruition: the work commenced has a completion date in view (v. 6). When we see the work of God in Jesus Christ in our own lives, it provokes joy, for it is grace alone that has called us and transforms us. Recognising the same work of grace in the experience of others stimulates wonder that 'all partakers with me of grace' (v. 7) are bound confidently by the same promises and the same timescale. The glory of the universal Church causes us and encourages us, along with Paul, to love those with whom we share in 'partnership in the gospel', in the 'defence and confirmation of the gospel' and in joyful thanksgiving to God.

Such is the glorious paradox of the Church. The glory of the hidden Church of God's holy people can only be revealed imperfectly, at best, in the church locally. Yet such a glorious understanding continues to provoke within us, in our own day, a yearning 'with the affection of Christ Jesus' (v. 8) for participation in that divine–human fellowship with his people.

3 Joy: prayer for abundance

Philippians 1:3–11

Paul knew, and his readers at Philippi appreciated, how much personal sacrifice was attached to identifying themselves publicly with the Lord Jesus Christ. They would surely have known that his first visit to Philippi followed a frustrating time for Paul. Opportunities to preach the gospel seemed to have been blocked by the Holy Spirit. The vision of the man of Macedonia calling Paul into Europe for the first time must have filled his heart with great expectations (Acts 16:9). After an early 'success' in the conversion of Lydia, however, much of the rest of his stay in Philippi was characterised by hardships—an unjust trial, beatings and an earthquake. The conversion of the Philippian jailer was followed by an appeal from the authorities for Paul and his companions to leave the city immediately (Acts 16:39).

Paul recognises how tenuous is the position of the heavenly colony at Philippi; his gratitude for their continuing participation in grace, during his imprisonment for the gospel, is deep (v. 7). Indeed, his thanksgiving is an outpouring of the 'affection of Christ Jesus' towards them (v. 8). Paul also recognises that increasing opposition and persecution will further challenge this small outpost of the empire of grace.

His prayer for the church is permeated with a recognition that in order for them to 'stand firm' (see 1: 27–28), a supernatural, abundant confidence will be required. He prays for a joyful, abundant and life-transforming love to overwhelm them. He intercedes that love—towards Jesus Christ and towards one another—might 'abound more and more', along with 'more and more knowledge and discernment' (v. 9). Knowledge in itself might well produce an informed people, but without genuine discernment the same divine knowledge might easily foster ungodly pride (1 Corinthians 8: 1–3). The true measure of knowledge and discernment is an approval of what is excellent, transforming and righteous. The expected completion date for the divine work commenced in Christ—namely, 'the day of Jesus Christ' (v. 6)—is also the timeline that Christians are to pursue in their growth in holiness (v. 10).

Thanksgiving characterises Paul's prayer at its outset (v. 3); at its summation, his desire remains that the glorious Church, made manifest locally in the church at Philippi, will be an abundant, informed, discerning, holy people, existing solely to the glory and praise of God (v. 11).

4 Joy in the household

Philippians 1:12–18

It is not difficult for any of us to imagine how troubled the small church at Philippi must have been by the news that Paul had been put under arrest in Rome. Even when Paul and Silas had been in Philippi, charges of sedition had been laid against them, saying that they were 'disturbing our peace [and] advocating customs that are not lawful to us' (Acts 16: 20–21).

In his letter to them, Paul, again following the literary conventions of his day, proceeds to offer *reassurance about the sender* (1:12–26). His reassurance to his partners in the gospel insists that neither external opposition nor opposition from troublesome elements within the church has been able to hinder the spread of the gospel message.

Paul does not make light of his circumstances in prison (1:13–14, 17), the wounds inflicted because of 'envy and rivalry', or the insincerity of those who seek to afflict his ministry (1:15, 17). Yet, in spite of these difficulties, the spread of the gospel continues apace.

The content of the gospel is centred on the work of God in the Lord Jesus Christ (1:2). Although he does refer to 'Jesus Christ' (1:6, 11), Paul's preferred means of referring to 'the Lord' (v. 14) is by the title 'Christ' (1:10, 13, 15, 17, 18). The Lord Jesus Christ might be regarded by Roman authorities as a weak challenger to their emperor's claims to lordship and divinity, but the reality is that Christ's Lordship does not depend on the assent of other mortals. Christ's divine appointment and nature cannot be confined either by external persecution or by weaknesses within the church. His kingship will grow and Caesar's will decline.

Paul's imprisonment has emboldened fearful Christians in Rome (v. 14). Even his 'opponents' are preaching Christ (v. 18) and, more astonishing still, 'the advance of the gospel' has continued even throughout Caesar's own imperial guard. Reports of his own conditions might have provided further discouragement to his partners, but Paul's joy-filled reflection on the circumstances of his imprisonment must have caused rejoicing among the Philippians, for 'all the saints' in Rome, 'especially those of Caesar's household' (4:22), are numbered among those who encourage them.

Neither external opposition nor internal disputes can hinder the growing kingdom that still awaits certain completion 'at the day of Jesus Christ' (v. 6).

5 Confidence and joy in Christ's glory

Philippians 1:18b–26

During their overnight imprisonment at Philippi (Acts 16:25–26), Paul and Silas must have astonished their fellow prisoners by singing songs of praise to God. The ensuing earthquake is not explained by any vocal deficiencies on the part of either Paul or Silas! We might, however, having meditated on today's passage, understand better the source of this joyful confidence.

Paul clearly appreciates the precariousness of his position. In need of 'deliverance' (v. 19), he is unsure whether his life will continue or whether death will interrupt his service (v. 22). Yet he does not seem to be overcome with confusion or stymied by fear. Elsewhere, Paul explains how he has been freed 'to live to God', insisting that 'I have been crucified with Christ. It is no longer I who live, but Christ who lives in me' (Galatians 2:19b–20). Having learned this grace-filled secret of self-forgetfulness, Paul can confirm to the Philippians his joyful hope that 'to live is Christ, and to die is gain' (v. 21). His desire, whether in life or death, in service or sacrifice, is overwhelmingly 'to be with Christ' (v. 23).

We might consider further grounds for Paul's joyful confidence. First, there is the partnership of Christian believers. Although he is alone in his imprisonment, he has not been abandoned (1:5–7). Their answered prayers will secure his release from prison, enabling further usefulness among them (v. 19) and resulting in their 'progress and joy in the faith' (v. 25). Ultimately, this will enable them together to 'glory in Christ' (1:11, 26).

Second, God's nature as Trinity is the ultimate source of his confidence. God the Father is recognised as the author of grace and peace (1:2); the focus of Christian experience is mediated through his Son (see vv. 19, 20, 21, 23, 26); and, by the indwelling help of the 'Spirit of Jesus Christ', hope ceases to be a philosophical concept and becomes a living, life-transform-ing, powerful, joy-filled confidence. God's plan will be completed in their lives (1:6, 10).

Third, despite hardships, serving Christ (expressed in his desire 'to be with Christ') has afforded Paul continuing joy (v. 18b). In spite of external opposition and internal tensions. Paul longs for his partners in the Philip-pian church, like himself, to 'progress', experiencing hope-filled 'joy in the faith' in the present, while anticipating the completion of God's glorious, grace-filled future at the day of Christ.

6 Joy-filled humility

Philippians 1:27—2:5

Having encouraged his readers with *news about the sender*, Paul seeks *reassurance about the recipient's affairs*. However, he does not limit himself to the formulaic conventions of his time, for he seeks information about their well-being in two parts of his letter (1:27—2:18; 3:1—4:3).

Recognising that their experience mirrors his own, facing opposition from the Roman authorities (compare 1:13 with 1:28a, 30) and tensions within the church (compare 1:15 with 2:3a), Paul directs them to consider four things as encouragements to live worthily of Christ: first, the character of the 'gospel of Christ' (1:27); second, the nature of discipleship 'for the sake of Christ' (v. 29); third, the pattern of 'encouragement in Christ' (2:1); and finally the 'mind… of Christ' (v. 5). Their ability to withstand the exter-nal and internal challenges to their communal life will be overcome as their lifestyle choices truly reflect their commitment of faith.

This unity is essentially a spiritual unity in Christ (Galatians 3:24–28), expressed by a common understanding of the 'gospel of Christ' and by a commitment to common endeavour for the sake of that same gospel (Philippians 1:27). Such unity is not only a 'worthy' lifestyle choice; it is the source of the strength that enables them to continue to 'stand' without fear when external opposition comes against them (v. 28). Their shared suffering with one another and with Paul (vv. 29–30) means standing in formation, almost like soldiers facing attack, 'for the sake of Christ' (v. 29). Such unity of spirit, mind and purpose carries before an antagonistic world a profound eschatological significance (v. 28).

While a common purpose, common understanding and united commitment develop strength to stand in the face of external opposition and internal tensions, a disunited church, disjointed and distrustful, will inevitably be weak in the face of opposition. So encouragement in Christ creates a glorious fellowship of faith. In 2:1–2 Paul notes how positive virtues might be adopted. Far from being fuzzy or weak virtues, these expressions of deep commitment actually create a body able to withstand external threats. Permitting negative traits such as selfishness, rivalry, pride or conceit to flourish will weaken and injure their testimony. Discerning and approving what is excellent and being filled with the fruit of righteousness (1:9–11) are ultimately about discovering and living the mind of Christ in fellowship with one another.

Guidelines

In pre-Beeching days, when small steam trains puffed and chuffed their way up and down the South Wales Valleys, calling at every platform and halt, the following conversation was overheard. One rather pompous passenger, annoyed by the continual stops, got out of her carriage and marched towards the driver.

'Driver!' she cried. 'Can't you go any faster?'

'Yes, madam,' came the reply, 'but I'm not allowed to leave the train.'

How many of us might express similar frustration with our local church or denominational structures? Have we ever been tempted to abandon the 'Church' because of our experience of the 'church'? How might our thoughts during the week about the glory of God's called people enable us to engage creatively with our local expression of church? How might Philippians 2:1–5 encourage us to value and serve our local fellowship joyfully?

Pray for your local church, giving thanks for it but also praying for people you find more difficult to relate to.

1 Joy in worship and service of the Lord

Philippians 2:5–18

Whether verses 5–11 were composed by Paul or by others, whether they comprise an early 'hymn' to Jesus or not, and how these verses should best be interpreted have been fruitful topics of discussion among Bible scholars. As one commentator helpfully observed, however, even if these questions could be finally resolved, Paul's record is the only form we have of the verses, and they need therefore to be taken seriously as part of the Pauline canon.

Two alternative suggestions about how these verses should be read will enable us to be caught up in the joyful worship befitting Christ's followers; such worship will also stimulate our joyful, humble service as we emulate Christ day by day.

One approach directs us to consider Christ as the second Adam. Adam (in the account of Genesis 2—3), in grasping to be 'as God', over-reached himself, 'fell' and not only brought about his own abasement and humiliation but led the whole of creation into 'bondage to decay' (Romans 8:20–23). Jesus, on the contrary, although he possessed divinity, 'humbled himself' even to death and was exalted by God as divine Lord.

The second suggested way of reading the text encourages us to consider how the inhabitants of a Roman colony might have understood their revolutionary message. In the Roman imperial cult, the glorification and deification of the emperor symbolised the far-reaching power and inherent violence of imposed Roman colonial rule. Christ, on the other hand, who is truly Lord, humbled himself and was exalted by God (see Isaiah 45:23). It is at the name of Jesus that every knee shall bow. His humility is the glory and the empire. All other lords, devoid of such authority, are, in reality, idolatrous usurpers.

It is with such a glorious vision of the humbled but exalted Lord that the Church is called to live. Expecting eschatological fulfilment of 'salvation' on the 'day of Christ' (1:6; 2:16), the believers are to work out the implications of their salvation, reliant on the Lord who is at work within their lives. Paul's partners are called to live blameless, Christ-reflecting lives by holding on to the word of life. Thus, whether life or death befalls them, they can learn to be 'glad and rejoice with me' (v. 18).

2 Joy of companionship

Philippians 2:12–30

Joy continues to dominate this letter, even as Paul continues to follow the literary conventions of his day. Having sought *reassurance about the recipients* (vv. 12–18), he moves naturally on to passing *information about intermediaries* to the church at Philippi (vv. 19–30). Epaphroditus was one of their own (v. 25) and, along with Timothy, had been charged with delivering the letter. Paul's gratitude for their past cooperation with him in the gospel (1:6) includes a recognition of their ongoing shared participation in 'the same conflict' (1:30). Whether he is present or absent (1:27; 2:12), whether he lives or whether his life is poured out in a sacrificial offering, he desires that they would continue to hold fast to the word of life. To live, for them, as for himself, is to live in joyful service to Christ.

Although Paul hopes to visit the Philippians once again (1:19, 26; 2:23–24), his present imprisonment means that, in the meantime, the visit of Timothy and the return of Epaphroditus will encourage them and enable them to truly 'rejoice with me' (v. 18). To a concerned relative, a message or phone call from the hospital cannot replace the news and reassurance of a trusted visitor. Similarly, not only will Timothy's visit on Paul's behalf encourage the church at Philippi, but also his news will, upon his return, cheer Paul.

Timothy is commended by Paul for his genuine concern for the church's welfare. After meeting Paul's mission team at Lystra during Paul's second missionary journey, Timothy was inducted into his European mission at Philippi (Acts 16), and the city has, as Paul knows, a warm place in Timothy's heart. Timothy, he says, is proven, tested and genuine (2:22: the image he uses suggests genuine rather than counterfeit coinage). He is like a son in the faith, belonging to the family of faith (2 Timothy 1:5–6) and a trusted co-servant of Christ (1:1; 2:22).

Epaphroditus is well known to the Philippian church, since he has represented the generosity of the church and has shared in Paul's concerns and in his ministry on their behalf. Here is not only a 'brother' in the family of faith, but a fellow worker, a brother in arms, a messenger and a minister alongside Paul himself (vv. 25–26).

3 Rejoice in the Lord

Philippians 3:1–11

Previously in this letter, Paul modelled joy when persecution from outside the church or disruptive elements within the church sought to 'afflict' him in his captivity. The Philippian church, facing 'the same' external and internal pressures, were encouraged, in eschatological hope, joyfully to worship and emulate the humble king whose vindication and Lordship brought glory to the Father. Continuing to rejoice in the Lord would strengthen them in the face of external threats and internal tensions.

Although verse 2 in this passage hints at some of the issues disturbing the church, attempts to identify the precise cause of tension have proved inconclusive. The Philippian church does not seem to have been troubled by the activities of a 'Judaising' party, as was the case in the Galatian churches. The temptation and tension at Philippi, one commentator suggests, were far subtler. In recognition of their monotheistic faith, Jewish synagogues had been exempted by the Romans from offering sacrifices to Caesar. Perhaps tensions had emerged in Philippi relating to the possibility of being 'circumcised' and thereby becoming 'Jews' in order to avoid persecution. For Paul, this course of action would smack of placing confidence in the flesh rather than submitting joyfully to the Lordship of Christ.

Paul directs his readers to ponder three aspects of glorying in Christ without resorting to having 'confidence in the flesh' (v. 3).

First, true faith in God is recognised by worship in the Spirit of God (see also John 4:24). Where Deuteronomy 30:6 foresaw abundant life as a consequence of worshipping God with heart and soul, the Christian, through the Spirit of God, glorifies Christ in his fullness now, and will inherit the completion of God's restorative promises for creation (Ephesians 1:12–14) through, and at, the resurrection.

Second, while not denigrating his race or heritage (vv. 3–4), Paul has considered and reevaluated the true worth of any 'righteousness' he might have been able to accrue. Righteousness is a gift of God through faith, leading to the completion of the work commenced at the day of Christ—that is, the resurrection—which is far, far better.

Third, to know Christ has all-surpassing worth (v. 8). A recognition of the conquering, vindicated Lord, who invites his people to participate in his righteousness and resurrection by faith, creates a desire within them, whatever the cost, to know Christ (v. 7), to gain Christ (v. 8) and to 'become' like Christ (v. 10). Such knowledge is what enables them to 'rejoice in the Lord' (v. 1).

4 Joy-filled, life-transforming hope

Philippians 3:12—4:1

Philippians 3 continues with the confidence and humility expressed previously (vv. 8–10). Humility recognises that 'righteousness', the life of Jesus now as well as the expectation of future resurrection, is incomplete. Perfect attainment, resurrection and complete knowledge have not yet been fully inherited. Confidence is a response to the grace of God in Christ Jesus. The Christ who began a good work in the believer's life (1:6–8), the knowledge of whom is life and in whose life death itself is gain (1:21), continually calls his people to work out their salvation in fear and trembling (2:12). To know him has 'surpassing worth' (3:7–8), for Christ will complete his perfecting work. The Christ who 'made me his own' has also become the prize.

To discern all this is an expression of shared maturity (vv. 15–16) and of shared co-imitation of the 'example' of faith. In an analogy taken from the race track, Paul's 'straining forward toward the goal' involves a deliberate 'forgetting what lies behind'—past achievements, past sins, past disappointments, past hurts—as well as a deliberate focus on the 'upward call' to know Christ finally and completely (compare 3:8–10, 14).

The 'straining forward' of the Christian life is then compared with the flabby, undisciplined, inconsistent 'walk' of the 'enemies of the cross of Christ' (vv. 18–19). Although Paul does not identify these enemies, he identifies their values and warns his readers to recognise the outcome of their lives. The end of their 'walk' is 'destruction', whereas the Christian believer's life is fulfilled in Christ himself. Serving the insatiable earthbound idols of human desires leads to disappointment and shame, whereas those who glory in Christ are directed by heavenly aspirations.

Finally (3:20—4:1), Paul adopts and subverts the titles and political propaganda of the Roman emperor himself to explain the revolutionary eschatological hope in Christ. The believers, as true citizens of heaven (3:20), are to live joyfully, expecting and anticipating the coming Saviour. Christ's limitless authority will, at his coming, complete his upward calling, by transforming their bodies to be like his own.

Their calling, as co-participants with this shared Saviour and shared hope, is to 'stand firm' (1:27; 4:1) and to 'agree in the Lord' in the face of external persecution and internal threats (4:2–3).

5 Joy and peace, peace and joy

Philippians 4:1–9

The 19th-century preacher F.B. Meyer observed, 'Peace is joy resting; joy is peace dancing.' Facing a future in which trials and persecution will threaten the church at Philippi, and fear and anxiety will be natural reactions, Paul encourages his 'crown and joy' to rejoice, for their names are written in the 'book of life' (v. 3; see Luke 10:20).

The double encouragement to 'rejoice in the Lord' (v. 4) grows from Paul's assurance of their hope in Christ, knowing 'the peace of God' and serving the 'God of peace'. Arguably, this paragraph summarises the overarching themes of the letter. Gordon Fee, in his commentary, observes that the first subsection (vv. 4–7) speaks about Christian piety, while the second (vv. 8–9) speaks of Christian ethical assumptions. The first reflects the piety of the Hebrew Bible, with a celebration of the Lord's holiness, righteousness, faithfulness and protection, and the believer's thirst after God and thanksgiving for his goodness. Here, though, its stimulus comes from a knowledge that the eschaton has been not only anticipated but also inaugurated. After all, 'the Lord is near' (v. 5). Prayer, petitions, thanksgiving and gentleness are all expressions of this piety. Anxiety is a denial of the transcendent peace of God. Worshipping and knowing Christ, like being within a Roman encampment protected by strong guards, protects our minds and hearts and is a foretaste of the final completed *shalom* of God.

Similarly, a knowledge that the 'God of peace' is with his people calls not only for an emulation of Paul's own teaching and practice (v. 9) but also for a transformed and transforming reappraisal of our values. The

Welsh word for 'culture' hints at this transforming imperative. *Diwylliant* means literally the 'un-wilding' of a person or an object, whether a field, a landscape, a mind, a life or a community. Recognising what is 'true' in Christ teaches us to value that which is 'honourable', while pondering that which is 'just' transforms our perception of what is 'pure'. That which we regard as 'lovely' will inevitably shape what we would want to commend to ourselves and to others. Such minds are drawn toward 'excellence' in the spiritual, cultural and practical ethical decisions of life. Independent of the views of contemporary morality, pondering Christ and all those things worthy of praise will inevitably have the effect of 'un-wilding' our lives.

6 Rejoicing at the provision of God

Philippians 4:10–23

As he concludes his letter, Paul follows literary conventions by *exchanging greetings with third parties* before *closing with a wish for good health*. After greeting the recipients, Paul started his letter by thanking the church at Philippi for their partnership (1:3–4) and sought to encourage them. After all, the good news of the true Lord Jesus Christ—his humility, death on the cross and subsequent glorification to the position of true Lordship, higher than any other authority (2:5–11)—had been heard right at the heart of government (1:13).

In concluding his letter, Paul seeks to encourage the church at Philippi once again. Philippi, the Roman colony, where symbols of imperial authority and the proclamation of Caesar's lordship abound, is now informed that not only has the gospel been preached and shared among the imperial guard but also 'the saints... of Caesar's household' wish to attach their greetings (v. 22).

The church at Philippi can rejoice over what their partnership has facilitated (4:15). Their concern has been practical as well as genuine. They have sent Epaphroditus to visit Paul in prison (2:25–28; 4:18) and have supported his ministry on numerous occasions. Paul, however, is wary of suggesting that his gratitude is in any way feigned or is an excuse to seek additional support (v. 11). Rather, he directs the Philippians' attention one more time to the thing he has taught and exemplified among them—that Christ himself is sufficient in life and in death.

Paul explains this in two ways. First, his personal testimony is directed toward the all-sufficiency of Christ (3:7–9). Being humbled or honoured, experiencing abundance or need—all are part of his experience, and all present a temptation to self-reliance. He has learned, whatever his external circumstances, that true joy comes from knowing Christ (vv. 11–13). Second, his partners in the gospel, whatever circumstances they may face, will also find their sufficiency in Christ. 'Every need' (v. 19) will be provided for by God, from the riches of Christ. Such abundance, such provision, such a Christ, such a gracious God alone is worthy of all 'glory' (vv. 19–20). And, as always, it is to the all-surpassing, unmerited grace of God that past blessings and future hope direct us: that grace will sustain us in the present.

Guidelines

We began the week by contemplating the glory of the humbled, crucified, exalted Lord. How might we move beyond a contemplation of this Lord—humble yet majestic, crucified yet glorified—to practice? What might it mean for us to work out our salvation in fear and trembling?

Throughout his letter to the Philippian Christians, Paul holds two apparently conflicting teachings in tension with one another. The sovereign, saving Lord has already come to his world, and his work as Saviour is glorious beyond measure, but it is, as yet, incomplete. To know him is far, far better than all else, but we are not yet able to know him completely. In our present struggles, our faith awaits a final consummation, when the Lord will return and transform even our lowly bodies to be like his glorious resurrection body. Both aspects are true: present experience and future hope confirm it. How might holding these truths in tension create, stimulate and confirm our faith in Christ each day?

In *The Last Battle*, the concluding volume in the 'Narnia Chronicles', C.S. Lewis explores the nature of the Christian life. The call to be in Christ, to live in Christ and grow towards Christ, is a continual exploration of known landscapes that are revealed more wonderfully and renewed constantly in the presence of the Christ. So the call to press on, 'further up and further in', is our daily calling. How might we go about pressing 'further up and further in' in our knowledge of Christ today?

What does it mean for us today to 'hold fast to the word of life' (Philippians 2:16)?

FURTHER READING

Moisés Silva, *Philippians* (Baker Exegetical Commentary), Baker Academic, 2005.

Peter T. O'Brien, *The Epistle to the Philippians: A commentary on the Greek text*, Eerdmans, 1991.

Markus Bockmuehl, *The Epistle to the Philippians* (Black's New Testament Commentaries), A&C Black, 1998.

Ben Witherington III, *Paul's Letter to the Philippians*, Eerdmans, 2011.

N.T. Wright, *Paul for Everyone: The prison letters*, SPCK, 2004.

Supporting Messy Church with a gift in your will

For many charities, income from legacies is crucial in enabling them to plan ahead, and often provides the funding to develop new projects. Legacies make a significant difference to the ability of charities to achieve their purpose. In just this way, a legacy to support BRF's ministry would make a huge difference.

One of the fastest growing areas of BRF is its Messy Church ministry (www.messychurch.org.uk). Messy Church is a form of church focused on building relationships, engaging with people outside the usual church context and building a Christ-centred community. Messy Church gives families and all age groups an opportunity to be together and is a congregation in its own right. In addition, it is being delivered in a variety of different contexts in local communities, including care homes, prisons, inner cities, schools and rural areas. Week by week we are seeing new Messy Churches starting up across the UK and around the globe, across all major Christian denominations. A conservative estimate is that over 400,000 people are attending Messy Church each month.

Throughout its history, BRF's ministry has been enabled thanks to the generosity of those who have shared its vision and supported its work, both by giving during their lifetime and also through legacy gifts.

A legacy gift would help fund the development and sustainability of BRF's Messy Church ministry into the future. We hope you may consider a legacy gift to help us continue to take this work forward in the decades to come.

For further information about making a gift to BRF in your will or to discuss how a specific bequest could be used to develop our ministry, please contact Sophie Aldred (Head of Fundraising) or Richard Fisher (Chief Executive) by email at fundraising@brf.org.uk or by phone on 01865 319700.

The BRF

Magazine

Celebrating ten years of *Quiet Spaces*

Karen Laister

Spirituality is seen as a journey by many people, and it would be true to say that our prayer and spirituality journal *Quiet Spaces* has been on a journey over these past ten years as it has evolved in both content and style.

When we first started discussing the possibility of a journal that would help people experience a relational approach to their faith, we struggled to find a name. It took us much debate to decide that 'Quiet Spaces' was what we wanted to provide for its readers. *Quiet Spaces* was born out of a recognition that we need to create space to grow our relationship with God, to spend time with him and learn spiritual disciplines that aid our reflection and contemplation. Becky Winter, the first editor of *Quiet Spaces*, talked about wanting people to 'know God rather than knowing about God'.

We also envisaged the journal being very different from our Bible reading notes. In fact, we saw it sitting alongside *New Daylight*, *Guidelines* and *Day by Day with God*, complementing their approach and providing material to develop a life of prayer.

With *Quiet Spaces* we wanted to enable give readers a starting point to explore different styles of Christian spirituality and provide approaches to enrich a life of prayer and spirituality. Initially *Quiet Spaces* was unstructured and readers could dip in and out as they wished. More recently we have provided a structure based on different themes to enable people to use the journal on a regular basis if they wish.

'Be still and know that I am God' (Psalm 46:10, NIV) is a call to stop and discover God. Some of us might be good at doing this, while others can't seem to find the time or, when we do, find our minds floating off in all kinds of directions. Making time, in many respects, is the starting point for our prayer or communion with God, when we still ourselves and invite God to be in those moments. *Quiet Spaces* provides readings, reflection, creativity and prayers to explore spirituality in the stillness of our soul and to begin to glimpse something of God.

Quiet Spaces might be something that you keep alongside your Bible and dip into over the course of a four-month issue. There might be material that you keep returning to because you have been moved by a reflection, prayer or poem. It has captured your attention and draws you back to explore more. The eight or nine sections in each edition allow you to plan some longer periods of quiet. We sometimes have to be intentional about carving out time away from the demands and the noise of life for space with God or to give ourselves some much-needed rest. It is when we stop and reflect that we gain perspective, seeing God alongside us in the difficult, the mundane or the times of joy.

Christian spirituality throughout the ages has used techniques to stop and reflect. The 'examen' is a Jesuit approach to reviewing the day. We might not have time to do this daily, but perhaps every couple of weeks we can look back at the ways we have seen God in our lives since we last stopped to examine our faith journey. Keeping a journal might be useful if you are using *Quiet Spaces* as a mini retreat. Reflecting on what has taken place in your life allows you to consider situations that have upset or pleased you, then to think about how you could have approached things differently and to invite God to journey with you.

Alongside *Quiet Spaces*, BRF runs a Quiet Day programme and organises a Festival of Prayer each year with Oxford Diocese. Learning and sharing with others provides encouragement and can be a very special time. For information about our Quiet Day programme, you can visit our website: www.quietspaces.org.uk.

At the beginning of this article, I wrote that *Quiet Spaces* has been on a journey since its launch ten years ago, and we are grateful to Becky Winter, Naomi Starkey, Heather Fenton and the current editor, Sally Smith, for bringing together writers who have such wide experience in different aspects of spirituality.

One reader wrote to us recently, 'Along with *Guidelines*, this year I ordered a copy of *Quiet Spaces*. At first I wondered how I would find time to read another set of devotions, but it is proving a wonderful resource and I am trying to limit how much I read in one session, otherwise it will be read within a couple of weeks! I find the themes really make me be still before God and meditate on his word.' Another reader wrote, 'It is simply brilliant. Format and content are excellent.'

We couldn't hope for better accolades to endorse *Quiet Spaces*. If you would like to try it, please visit www.biblereadingnotes.org.uk/quiet-spaces/ and click on 'Order a sample copy'. Then enter the promotion code QSSAMPLE at the checkout. Alternatively, contact the BRF office on 01865 319700 to order your free sample, quoting QSSAMPLE.

Karen Laister is Deputy Chief Executive of BRF.

BRF needs your help!

Sophie Aldred

Over the past decade or so, BRF's charitable activities have expanded from publishing Bible reading notes and books into exciting new and complementary areas such as the Barnabas in Schools programme, Messy Church and, most recently, The Gift of Years.

BRF's charitable activities resource:

- Christian growth and the understanding of the Bible by individuals of all ages
- churches for outreach in the local community
- the teaching of Christianity and the Bible within primary schools
- children's and family ministry in churches

Our main priority is to make what we have to offer widely accessible, and to make a difference in the lives of individuals, communities, schools and churches. BRF's charitable activities are funded partly through income generated from sales of resources and fees from training and events, and partly through voluntary income from donations, grants and legacies.

The following specific activities are funded primarily by donations, grants and legacies:

Messy Church

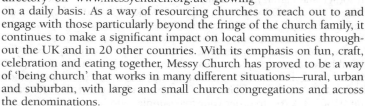

The Messy Church network continues to expand, with the number of Messy Churches listed in the directory on www.messychurch.org.uk growing on a daily basis. As a way of resourcing churches to reach out to and engage with those particularly beyond the fringe of the church family, it continues to make a significant impact on local communities throughout the UK and in 20 other countries. With its emphasis on fun, craft, celebration and eating together, Messy Church has proved to be a way of 'being church' that works in many different situations—rural, urban and suburban, with large and small church congregations and across the denominations.

Who Let The Dads Out?

Who Let The Dads Out?'s vision is to 'turn the hearts of fathers to their children and the hearts of children to their fathers' (Malachi 4:6). It is an extremely effective way for churches to engage with fathers and father figures of pre-school-aged children—particularly those with whom the church has very little, if any, contact. Who Let The Dads Out? groups across the UK are providing a vital catalyst for churches to engage with fathers and father figures, and a context to begin to explore issues and questions around fatherhood and faith.

The Gift of Years

The Gift of Years is BRF's newest initiative, which we started to develop in 2014. In recent years, Debbie Thrower (former BBC and ITV journalist and presenter) has developed a highly effective model for community-based 'Anna Chaplaincy' to older people in Alton, Hampshire. BRF enbraced the 'Anna Chaplain' model as the centrepiece of a new ministry, The Gift of Years, whose vision is 'resourcing the spiritual journey of older people'. Through this we are seeking both to resource older people themselves and also to resource ministry among older people, wherever they may be—in congregations, in residential care, in their own homes and in the community.

Barnabas in Schools

Barnabas in Schools is a professional education service to primary schools, helping teachers and pupils alike to explore Christianity and the Bible creatively within RE and Collective Worship. We do this through Barnabas RE Days, specialist In-Service Training (INSET) sessions for teachers, published resources for the classroom, and a website providing a wealth of support materials and ideas available to download. We estimate that the team works with 45,000 primary school children each year. Funding for RE is very limited in many primary schools, so the fees for Barnabas RE Days and INSET sessions are set at a level to make them as affordable as possible.

Foundations21

Foundations21 (www.foundations21.net) is BRF's free online Christian lifelong learning resource, offering a wealth of material to explore and enabling individuals and small groups to grow in their faith and discipleship. We continue to develop and refine this resource, and are currently working on an entry-level Christian learning app for tablet and mobile phone users.

Barnabas in Churches

For 20 years BRF has been resourcing ministry among children and families in churches through our websites and published resources, enabling children under 11, and the adults that work  with them, to explore Christianity creatively and bring the Bible alive. The Barnabas in Churches website (www.barnabasinchurches.org.uk) provides a wealth of free downloadable ideas for children's leaders to use with their Sunday or midweek groups, alongside the wide range of books published under our Barnabas for Children imprint to resource, equip and inspire them in their ministry.

Faith in Homes

Through our Faith in Homes initiative and its website, we are helping families to explore the Christian faith and to find God in the everyday at home, with ideas, articles, advice, published resources and workshops. Visit www.faithinhomes.org.uk.

Could you help us?

Messy Church, Who Let The Dads Out?, The Gift of Years, Barnabas in Schools, Foundations21, Barnabas in Churches and Faith in Homes are all funded primarily through donations, grants and legacies. We need your help to continue the growth and development of BRF's work in these areas.

Ways you could help:
- Give a personal donation (see page 151 for further details)
- Encourage your church to support BRF as part of its regular giving
- Make a legacy gift to BRF in your will
- Pray for everyone involved in BRF: the trustees and the staff team

Sophie Aldred is Head of Fundraising at BRF.

Recommended reading

Kevin Ball

Why do you read books? To escape, to learn? To deepen your faith? For me, the beauty of books is the way they show you new sides to a coin, opening up new possibilities and new understanding.

Tony Horsfall's new book, *Deep Calls to Deep*, asks, 'Is suffering an inescapable part of the journey towards knowing God?' It's tough, but true, that faith is shown for what it is in the hardest times, the messy times of life. Tony looks at the psalms of lament, songs that were written in the tough times, to see how the writers work through their messy life situations in a way that strengthens and develops their faith. You can read an extract from the book in the following pages.

What new understanding for our faith can we find in football? Who Let The Dads Out? founder Mark Chester reflects on the beautiful game, his family's love of Liverpool FC and his stuttering attempts to become a professional (well—good amateur!) player as he invites you to train with him (reflectively, that is) to discover the soul of the game.

How do I discover my true vocation? That's the question at the heart of Katy Magdalene Price's new book, *I Think It's God Calling*. Through her amusing and witty style, Katy shares her true story of how she discovered that God was calling her to ordained ministry, even though she struggled to believe in God.

For those in church leadership, we are pleased to be publishing *Pioneering a New Future* from the Archbishops' Missioner and Fresh Expressions Team Leader, Canon Phil Potter. Phil helps leaders to understand the changing church scene, with the emerging and growth of fresh expressions of church, charting a positive course through change to embrace these new missional possibilities. This is a revised and updated edition of *The Challenge of Change*, which we published in 2009.)

You can read sample chapters from all of the books described below at www.brfonline.org.uk.

Deep Calls to Deep
Spiritual formation in the hard places of life
Tony Horsfall

Tony explains his interest in the psalms of lament and their usefulness in spiritual formation.

It seems to me that the book of Psalms, when taken as a whole, provides us with a wonderful handbook on spiritual formation. Here we see life with God as it really is. True, there is a certain distance between us and the psalms—historically, geographically, culturally and even theologically, as they reflect the old covenant between God and his people. Not everything we read sits easily with a contemporary Western mindset. They are both familiar and foreign to us, yet they continue to speak deeply to us about our relationship with God. As one Old Testament professor puts it:

As we read the Psalms, we are entering into the sanctuary, the place where God meets men and women in a special way. We will see that the conversation between God and his people is direct, intense, intimate, and above all, honest. Thus, the Psalms are a kind of literary sanctuary in the Scripture. The place where God meets his people in a special way, where his people may address him with their praise and lament.'

It was this intimacy with God, this raw honesty with him, that drew me to the psalms in a fresh way. They give us words to use with God in our moments of joy and victory (praise) and in our times of despair and defeat (lament). As we read them, we can make the words our own, enter into the experience of the writer and find our own voice before God. In particular, I was drawn to the songs of lament, prayers that come from a deep place and reflect the struggle to understand what God is doing in our lives.

These 'sad songs' make up nearly a third of all the psalms and yet they are mostly neglected by the church today. Much of our spirituality is geared toward relieving our pain and finding ways to ensure happiness, success and well-being... Yet struggle and challenge are necessary for authentic spiritual growth. The reality is that God sometimes does lead us down difficult paths as he seeks to draw us closer to himself and form his life within us...

978 1 84101 731 0, pb, 160 pages, £7.99

I Think It's God Calling
A vocation diary
Katy Magdalene Price

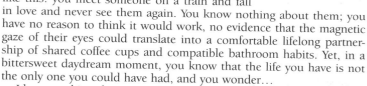

Katy shares the emotional and spiritual ups and downs of her calling to the priesthood, as well as the challenges for family and friends arising from such a major life change.

Vocation is a malady that runs its course differently in different people... For me, it felt a bit like this: you meet someone on a train and fall in love and never see them again. You know nothing about them; you have no reason to think it would work, no evidence that the magnetic gaze of their eyes could translate into a comfortable lifelong partnership of shared coffee cups and compatible bathroom habits. Yet, in a bittersweet daydream moment, you know that the life you have is not the only one you could have had, and you wonder...

I knew nothing about priesthood... Priesthood was not an ambition, a plan or even a desire; it was the last thing I wanted... But somehow all the sensible answers sounded false. It was also getting increasingly hard to hide from other people. People you'd never expect seemed to be picking up on some 'vibe'. A jolly homeless guy who usually spoke in a succession of unintelligible bad puns broke into what sounded like prophecy. Even my mother, who had finally given up her long-cherished hope that I would become a writer (hi Mum!), tentatively suggested that I might make a career out of being 'interested in religion'...

978 1 84101 645 0, pb, 176 pages, £7.99

The Soul of Football
One man's story of football, family and faith
Mark Chester

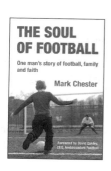

Cloning Jamie Carragher, Lionel Messi's mistakes and 'It's all Wayne Rooney's fault' are just three of the issues Mark reflects on as he shares his love of all things things footy and how love for the beautiful game can help football fans begin to discover the victory of a Christian faith. Mark writes:

It was a dream I shared with the vast majority of other boys and men. The dream was fuelled by Subbuteo and *Match of the Day*, by Panini stickers and *Football Focus*, by *Match* magazine and football cards with flat, rigid pieces of bubble gum so sharp you could cut yourself if you put them into your mouth at the wrong angle. But most of all, it was a dream fuelled by a man called Roy Race of Melchester Rovers...

'This book gets beyond the surface of football, and reminds us that we need to get beyond the surface of life, too.' (Revd John K. Boyers, Chaplain, Manchester United)

978 1 84101 654 2, pb, 112 pages, £6.99

Pioneering a new future
A guide to shaping change and changing the shape of church
Phil Potter

Change can be a frightening thing, particularly for leaders and congregations not fully prepared for what it will mean. The author of *The Challenge of Cell Church*, which has sold over 10,000 copies, returns in this revised edition of *The Challenge of Change*, offering a map for healthy and godly change in the local church. Writing as a pastor and practitioner, Phil explains ways of shaping change of any kind in the life of a church and presents a guide to understanding the changing shape of church, in particular the 'fresh expressions' of church now emerging. He uses his experiences of leading his own church through five major transition periods, with his own mistakes and personal stories as examples to illustrate his points.

Pioneering a New Future is ideal for church leaders of any denomination wanting to take their congregations through change. It is also ideal for church members preparing to embark on a particular project or simply wanting to be equipped for whatever lies ahead. It speaks to reluctant traditionalists and impatient visionaries, to both struggling and thriving congregations. Also included are over 100 questions for personal and group reflection.

978 0 85746 414 9, pb, 176 pages, £7.99 (available September 2015)

To order copies of any of these books, please turn to the order form on page 155, or visit www.brfonline.org.uk.

SUPPORTING BRF'S MINISTRY

As a Christian charity, BRF is involved in eight complementary areas.

- **BRF** (www.brf.org.uk) resources adults for their spiritual journey through Bible reading notes, books and Quiet Days. BRF also provides the infrastructure that supports our other specialist ministries.
- **Foundations21** (www.foundations21.net) provides flexible and innovative ways for individuals and groups to explore their Christian faith and discipleship through a multimedia internet-based resource.
- **Messy Church** (www.messychurch.org.uk), led by Lucy Moore, enables churches all over the UK (and increasingly abroad) to reach children and adults beyond the fringes of the church.
- **Barnabas in Churches** (www.barnabasinchurches.org.uk) helps churches to support, resource and develop their children's ministry with the under-11s more effectively .
- **Barnabas in Schools** (www.barnabasinschools.org.uk) enables primary school children and teachers to explore Christianity creatively and bring the Bible alive within RE and Collective Worship.
- **Faith in Homes** (www.faithinhomes.org.uk) supports families to explore and live out the Christian faith at home.
- **Who Let The Dads Out** (www.wholetthedadsout.org) inspires churches to engage with dads and their pre-school children.
- **The Gift of Years** (www.brf.org.uk/thegiftofyears) celebrates the blessings of long life and seeks to meet the spiritual needs of older people.

At the heart of BRF's ministry is a desire to equip adults and children for Christian living—helping them to read and understand the Bible, explore prayer and grow as disciples of Jesus. We need your help to make an impact on the local church, local schools and the wider community.

- You could support BRF's ministry with a one-off gift or regular donation (using the response form on page 153).
- You could consider making a bequest to BRF in your will.
- You could encourage your church to support BRF as part of your church's giving to home mission—perhaps focusing on a specific area of our ministry, or a particular member of our Barnabas team.
- Most important of all, you could support BRF with your prayers.

If you would like to discuss how a specific gift or bequest could be used in the development of our ministry, please phone 01865 319700 or email enquiries@brf.org.uk.

Whatever you can do or give, we thank you for your support.

HOW TO ENCOURAGE BIBLE READING IN YOUR CHURCH

BRF has been helping individuals connect with the Bible for over 90 years. We want to support churches as they seek to encourage church members into regular Bible reading.

Order a Bible reading resources pack

This pack is designed to give your church the tools to publicise our Bible reading notes. It includes:

- Sample Bible reading notes for your congregation to try.
- Publicity resources, including a poster.
- A church magazine feature about Bible reading notes.

The pack is free, but we welcome a £5 donation to cover the cost of postage. If you require a pack to be sent outside the UK or require a specific number of sample Bible reading notes, please contact us for postage costs. More information about what the current pack contains is available on our website.

How to order and find out more

- Visit **www.biblereadingnotes.org.uk/for-churches/**
- Telephone BRF on 01865 319700 between 9.15 am and 5.30 pm.
- Write to us at BRF, 15 The Chambers, Vineyard, Abingdon, OX14 3FE

Keep informed about our latest initiatives

We are continuing to develop resources to help churches encourage people into regular Bible reading, wherever they are on their journey. Join our email list at **www.biblereadingnotes.org.uk/helpingchurches/** to stay informed about the latest initiatives that your church could benefit from.

Introduce a friend to our notes

We can send information about our notes and current prices for you to pass on. Please contact us.

BRF is a Registered Charity

GL0215

BRF MINISTRY APPEAL RESPONSE FORM

I want to help BRF by funding some of its core ministries. Please use my gift for:

☐ Where most needed   ☐ Barnabas Children's Ministry   ☐ Foundations21
☐ Messy Church   ☐ Who Let The Dads Out?   ☐ The Gift of Years

Please complete all relevant sections of this form and print clearly.

Title _____ First name/initials _____ Surname _____
Address _____
_____ Postcode _____
Telephone _____ Email _____

Regular giving

If you would like to give by direct debit, please tick the box below and fill in details:

☐ I would like to make a regular gift of £ _____ per month / quarter / year
(delete as appropriate) by Direct Debit. (Please complete the form on page 159.)

If you would like to give by standing order, please contact Debra McKnight (tel: 01865 319700; email debra.mcknight@brf.org.uk; write to BRF address).

One-off donation

Please accept my special gift of

☐ £10 ☐ £50 ☐ £100 (other) £ _____ by

☐ Cheque / Charity Voucher payable to 'BRF'
☐ Visa / Mastercard / Charity Card
(delete as appropriate)

Name on card _____

Card no. ☐☐☐☐ ☐☐☐☐ ☐☐☐☐ ☐☐☐☐

Start date ☐☐☐   Expiry date ☐☐☐

Security code ☐☐☐

Signature _____ Date _____

☐ I would like to give a legacy to BRF. Please send me further information.

☐ I want BRF to claim back tax on this gift.
(If you tick this box, please fill in gift aid declaration overleaf.)

Please detach and send this completed form to: BRF, 15 The Chambers, Vineyard, Abingdon OX14 3FE.

BRF is a Registered Charity (No.233280)

GIFT AID DECLARATION

Bible Reading Fellowship

Please treat as Gift Aid donations all qualifying gifts of money made
today ☐   in the past 4 years ☐   in the future ☐   (tick all that apply)

I confirm I have paid or will pay an amount of Income Tax and/or Capital Gains Tax for each tax year (6 April to 5 April) that is at least equal to the amount of tax that all the charities that I donate to will reclaim on my gifts for that tax year. I understand that other taxes such as VAT or Council Tax do not qualify. I understand the charity will reclaim 25p of tax on every £1 that I give on or after 6 April 2008.

Donor's details

Title _____ First name or initials _____ Surname _____

Full home address _____

_____

Postcode _____

Date _____

Signature _____

Please notify Bible Reading Fellowship if you:

* want to cancel this declaration
* change your name or home address
* no longer pay sufficient tax on your income and/or capital gains.

If you pay Income Tax at the higher or additional rate and want to receive the additional tax relief due to you, you must include all your Gift Aid donations on your Self-Assessment tax return or ask HM Revenue and Customs to adjust your tax code.

GL0215

BRF PUBLICATIONS ORDER FORM

Please send me the following book(s):

		Quantity	Price	Total
731 0	Deep Calls to Deep (T. Horsfall)	_____	£7.99	_____
645 0	I Think It's God Calling (K. Magdalene Price)	_____	£7.99	_____
654 2	The Soul of Football (M. Chester)	_____	£6.99	_____
414 9	Pioneering a New Future (P. Potter)	_____	£7.99	_____
323 4	Living Liturgies (C. George)	_____	£7.99	_____
413 2	The Gift of Years (Bible reading notes)	_____	£2.50	_____
	Quiet Spaces sample copy	_____	FREE	_____

Total cost of books £ _____
Donation £ _____
Postage and packing £ _____
TOTAL £ _____

POSTAGE AND PACKING CHARGES				
Order value	UK	Europe	Economy (Surface)	Standard (Air)
Under £7.00	£1.25	£3.00	£3.50	£5.50
£7.00–£29.00	£2.25	£5.50	£6.50	£10.00
£30.00 and over	free	prices on request		

Please complete the payment details below and send with payment to: **BRF, 15 The Chambers, Vineyard, Abingdon OX14 3FE**

Name _____

Address _____

_____ Postcode _____

Tel _____ Email _____

Total enclosed £ _____ (cheques should be made payable to 'BRF')

Please charge my Visa ❑ Mastercard ❑ Switch card ❑ with £ _____

Card no: [ ][ ][ ][ ][ ][ ][ ][ ][ ][ ][ ][ ][ ][ ][ ][ ][ ][ ]

Expires [ ][ ][ ][ ] Security code [ ][ ][ ]

Issue no (Switch only) [ ][ ][ ]

Signature (essential if paying by credit/Switch) _____

_____

GUIDELINES INDIVIDUAL SUBSCRIPTIONS

❏ I would like to take out a subscription myself:

Your name _____

Your address _____

_____ Postcode _____

Tel _____ Email _____

Please send *Guidelines* beginning with the September 2015 / January 2016 / May 2016 issue: (delete as applicable)

(please tick box)	UK	Europe/Economy	Standard
GUIDELINES	❏ £16.35	❏ £24.00	❏ £27.60
GUIDELINES 3-year sub	❏ £42.75		

Please complete the payment details below and send with appropriate payment to: **BRF, 15 The Chambers, Vineyard, Abingdon OX14 3FE**

Total enclosed £ _____ (cheques should be made payable to 'BRF')

Please charge my Visa ❏ Mastercard ❏ Switch card ❏ with £ _____

Card no: ☐☐☐☐ ☐☐☐☐ ☐☐☐☐ ☐☐☐☐ ☐☐☐☐

Expires ☐☐☐☐ Security code ☐☐☐

Issue no (Switch only) ☐☐☐☐

Signature (essential if paying by card) _____

To set up a direct debit, please also complete the form on page 159 and send it to BRF with this form.

BRF is a Registered Charity

GL0215

GUIDELINES GIFT SUBSCRIPTIONS

❏ I would like to give a gift subscription (please provide both names and addresses:

Your name _____

Your address _____

_____ Postcode _____

Tel _____ Email _____

Gift subscription name _____

Gift subscription address _____

_____ Postcode _____

Gift message (20 words max. or include your own gift card for the recipient)

_____

_____

Please send *Guidelines* beginning with the September 2015 / January 2016 / May 2016 issue: (delete as applicable)

(please tick box)

	UK	Europe/Economy	Standard
GUIDELINES	❏ £16.35	❏ £24.00	❏ £27.60
GUIDELINES 3-year sub	❏ £42.75		

Please complete the payment details below and send with appropriate payment to: **BRF, 15 The Chambers, Vineyard, Abingdon OX14 3FE**

Total enclosed £ _____ (cheques should be made payable to 'BRF')

Please charge my Visa ❏ Mastercard ❏ Switch card ❏ with £ _____

Card no: ☐☐☐☐ ☐☐☐☐ ☐☐☐☐ ☐☐☐☐ ☐☐☐☐

Expires ☐☐☐☐ Security code ☐☐☐

Issue no (Switch only) ☐☐☐☐

Signature (essential if paying by card) _____

To set up a direct debit, please also complete the form on page 159 and send it to BRF with this form.

GL0215

DIRECT DEBIT PAYMENTS

Now you can pay for your annual subscription to BRF notes using Direct Debit. You need only give your bank details once, and the payment is made automatically every year until you cancel it. If you would like to pay by Direct Debit, please use the form opposite, entering your BRF account number under 'Reference'.

You are fully covered by the Direct Debit Guarantee:

The Direct Debit Guarantee

- This Guarantee is offered by all banks and building societies that accept instructions to pay Direct Debits.
- If there are any changes to the amount, date or frequency of your Direct Debit, The Bible Reading Fellowship will notify you 10 working days in advance of your account being debited or as otherwise agreed. If you request The Bible Reading Fellowship to collect a payment, confirmation of the amount and date will be given to you at the time of the request.
- If an error is made in the payment of your Direct Debit, by The Bible Reading Fellowship or your bank or building society, you are entitled to a full and immediate refund of the amount paid from your bank or building society.
  - – If you receive a refund you are not entitled to, you must pay it back when The Bible Reading Fellowship asks you to.
- You can cancel a Direct Debit at any time by simply contacting your bank or building society. Written confirmation may be required. Please also notify us.

The Bible Reading Fellowship

Instruction to your bank or building society to pay by Direct Debit

Please fill in the whole form using a ballpoint pen and send to The Bible Reading Fellowship, 15 The Chambers, Vineyard, Abingdon OX14 3FE.

Service User Number: | 5 | 5 | 8 | 2 | 2 | 9 |

Name and full postal address of your bank or building society

To: The Manager	Bank/Building Society
Address	
	Postcode

Name(s) of account holder(s)

Branch sort code

Bank/Building Society account number

Reference

Instruction to your Bank/Building Society

Please pay The Bible Reading Fellowship Direct Debits from the account detailed in this instruction, subject to the safeguards assured by the Direct Debit Guarantee.
I understand that this instruction may remain with The Bible Reading Fellowship and, if so, details will be passed electronically to my bank/building society.

Signature(s)
Date

Banks and Building Societies may not accept Direct Debit instructions for some types of account.

This page is intentionally left blank.